Enabling Inclusion:

Blue Skies ... Dark Clouds?

Enabling Inclusion

Blue Skies ... Dark Clouds?

Edited by Tim O'Brien

London: The Stationery Office

Applications for reproduction should be made in writing to The Stationery Office Limited, St Crispins, Duke Street, Norwich NR3 1PD.

The information contained in this publication is believed to be correct at the time of manufacture. Whilst care has been taken to ensure that the information is accurate, the publisher can accept no responsibility for any errors or omissions or for changes to the details given.

A CIP catalogue record for this book is available from the British Library

First published 2001

ISBN 0 11 702567 4

Printed in the United Kingdom by Albert Gait Ltd, Grimsby
TJ3674 C10 6/01

Published by The Stationery Office and available from:

The Stationery Office
(mail, telephone and fax orders only)
PO Box 29, Norwich NR3 1GN
General enquiries/Telephone orders 0870 600 5522
Fax orders 0870 600 5533

www.thestationeryoffice.com
www.schoolmanager.net

The Stationery Office Bookshops
123 Kingsway, London WC2B 6PQ
020 7242 6393 Fax 020 7242 6394
68–69 Bull Street, Birmingham B4 6AD
0121 236 9696 Fax 0121 236 9699
33 Wine Street, Bristol BS1 2BQ
0117 926 4306 Fax 0117 929 4515
9–21 Princess Street, Manchester M60 8AS
0161 834 7201 Fax 0161 833 0634
16 Arthur Street, Belfast BT1 4GD
028 9023 8451 Fax 028 9023 5401
The Stationery Office Oriel Bookshop
18–19 High Street, Cardiff CF1 2BZ
029 2039 5548 Fax 029 2038 4347
71 Lothian Road, Edinburgh EH3 9AZ
0870 606 5566 Fax 0870 606 5588

The Stationery Office's Accredited Agents
(see Yellow Pages)

and through good booksellers

Contents

Contents

Contents

Contents

List of figures and tables

Figures

Tables

Contributors

Mike Blamires Principal Lecturer in Education, Special Needs Research and Development Unit, Centre for Educational Research, Canterbury Christ Church University College.

John Cornwall Senior Lecturer in Education, Special Needs Research and Development Unit, Centre for Educational Research, Canterbury Christ Church University College.

Jean B. Crockett Professor of Education Management (Learning Disabilities), University of Virginia, United States of America.

Charles Gains Freelance writer, editor and lecturer. Formerly editor of 'Support for Learning'.

Philip Garner Professor of Special Needs Education, Nottingham Trent University.

Garry Hornby Senior Lecturer in Special Needs Education, University of Hull.

Marie Howley Lecturer in Special Needs Education, Northampton University College.

Roger Kidd Former Head of East Riding Learning Support Service.

Tim O'Brien Lecturer in Psychology Learning and Human Development, Institute of Education, University of London.

Sue Pearson Lecturer in Education, University of Leeds. Formerly President of NASEN.

Christopher Robertson Lecturer in Education, University of Birmingham.

Richard Rose Principal Lecturer in Special Needs Education, Northampton University College.

Janet Tod Reader in Education, Special Needs Research and Development Unit, Centre for Educational Research, Canterbury Christ Church University College.

Introduction

This book has its origins in a symposium that was organised at Canterbury Christ Church University College, Kent, in March 2000. The chapters in this book are revised versions of the papers that were presented at the symposium.

The authors have taken positional stances regarding inclusion and conceptualise inclusion within an 'enabling' framework. All of the authors are committed to creating an inclusive learning community – which extends into the wider community beyond school – however, they recognise that there are some dark clouds within the blue skies of inclusion. The idealism that can, at times, be associated with inclusion is unhelpful in improving provision in schools. After all, the ultimate winners or losers are the key stakeholders – individual learners: often with additional educational needs, teachers, parents and advocates. If the main stakeholders perceive changes as being a combination of externally imposed ideals with inevitable impractical outcomes, then the development of practice will be severely restricted.

If we are to increase the success of inclusion, questions about its meaning, nature and direction have to be confronted. Uncontested theories have to be challenged and provision analysed and evaluated. This is why inclusion is an exciting educational reform. It offers opportunities to engage in long-term professional discussion, to place practice under constant review, and to promote reflection and development. It also offers opportunities to involve learners, parents and teachers in the decision-making process.

Inclusion cannot become a concept so venerated that the moral standpoints of people are called into question if they scrutinize or challenge the assumptions, values and models that are associated with it. If inclusion is to benefit all learners, as every author in this book would want it to, we have to engage in a more thorough critical debate. The following chapters are intended to both stimulate and contribute to this debate

Tim O'Brien

Garry Hornby

1.1 Introduction

Providing service delivery to special education students has been fraught with controversy about which students should be served, which curricula and instructional methodologies should be used, and where instruction should be provided (Crockett and Kauffman, 1999). At present, two of the most controversial policy issues in the field of special needs education are the inclusion of increasing numbers of children with special educational needs (SEN) in mainstream schools and the high level of exclusions of children with disruptive behaviour (DfEE, 1997, 1998; Hornby, 1999; Hornby *et al.*, 1997). It is ironic that writers in the field of special education have so far paid more attention to children with learning difficulties in special schools who could be included in mainstream schools, than to those children with SEN who are being excluded from mainstream schools because of behavioural difficulties. Many of the latter end up not attending school at all.

While most educators are in favour of including as many children as possible in mainstream schools, there is widespread concern about the campaign by some writers (e.g. Ainscow, 1997) and organisations (e.g. Centre for the Studies of Inclusive Education, 1989) to bring about 'full inclusion', which involves all children with SEN spending most of their time in age-appropriate regular classes in their neighbourhood schools. The Salamanca Statement on inclusion is often cited in support of this view. As O'Brien has stated: *'The impetus behind the Salamanca statement (UNESCO, 1994) has resulted in what can, at times, appear to be a tidal wave of inclusive intent preached with overpowering zeal by the church of inclusion.'* This apparent obsession with the inclusion of some children with SEN, and the corresponding lack of attention to the exclusion of others (apparent in much recent special education literature), is considered to have come about because of various confusions which are evident at present in the field of special education. These confusions on definitions, rights, aetiology, curriculum, goals, reality, finance, means/ends, labelling and treatment models, are discussed in this chapter.

1998, p. 151

1.2 Inclusion Confusions

1.2.1 Definition

First and foremost there is confusion about what is meant by 'inclusion', as the term is used in various ways, 'inclusive schools' and 'inclusive society' being examples. The Green Paper (DfEE, 1997) talks about increasing inclusion by increasing the numbers of children with SEN in mainstream schools while maintaining special schools for those who need them. In contrast, CSIE (1989) uses inclusion to describe a state of affairs in which all children are educated in mainstream classes within mainstream schools with only temporary withdrawal from this situation envisaged. This is generally termed full inclusion. In addition, many inclusionists (e.g. Ainscow, 1997) speak of inclusion as a process. This process involves whole school re-organisation in order to develop inclusive schools. Implicit in this process, however, is the eventual goal of full inclusion. Also, the term social inclusion is used to refer to the goal of bringing about an inclusive society, which is one in which all individuals are valued and have important roles to play. Since the word inclusion is used in so many different ways it is important, in order to avoid confusion, to be clear about what is meant by the term. While the majority of people involved in education are in favour of inclusive schools, which include most children with SEN, many have reservations about full inclusion – which envisages all children with SEN being educated in mainstream classes.

1.2.2 Rights

The most important confusion concerns the rights of children with SEN. A powerful argument put forward in favour of full inclusion is that it is a basic human right of all children to be educated in their neighbourhood school with their mainstream peers. To segregate children for any reason is considered to be a denial of their human rights by many inclusionists. However, there are two main confusions here. First of all, there is confusion between human rights and moral rights. Just because someone has a human right to a certain option does not necessarily mean that it is morally the right thing for them to do (Thomson, 1990). Thus, although their human rights allow children with SEN to be educated alongside their mainstream peers, for some of them this may not, morally, be the right option. Kauffman asks:

Under what conditions, if any, is an approach to education 'right' even if it doesn't work? Can education or treatment be morally 'right' if it provides no benefit, even if it does harm? Are we to assume that what is 'right' for most students is 'right' for all, regardless of benefit or harm in the individual case?

1992, p. v

A second aspect of the 'rights' confusion concerns priorities. As well as their right to be included, children also have a right to an appropriate education suited to their needs. Surely the right to an appropriate education which meets pupils' specific needs is more important than the right to be educated alongside their neighbourhood peers (Lindsay, 1997)? It cannot be defensible to include all children in mainstream schools if this means that some of them will not be able to receive the education most appropriate for their special educational needs. Likewise, it is not defensible to exclude children from mainstream schools unless other specialist provision is available to ensure that their right to an appropriate education is not denied.

1.2.3 Aetiology

An important confusion which is creating problems in the field of SEN at present concerns theories about the aetiology of SEN. Until around three decades ago it was assumed that SEN resulted entirely from physiological or psychological difficulties inherent in children themselves. In the past thirty years awareness has grown concerning just how much social and environmental factors can influence children's functioning (Bronfenbrenner, 1979). This has been useful in making teachers aware of their potential roles in increasing or reducing the numbers of children experiencing SEN through the teaching and organisational strategies which are used in schools. However, some inclusionists have taken this social perspective to its extreme and suggest that SEN are entirely socially constructed. They suggest that it is teachers who have special needs, which are to learn ways of adapting the curriculum and their teaching methods in order to cater for the wide range of abilities and difficulties which pupils exhibit. The implication of this is that mainstream schools should be able to adapt in order to meet the needs of all children with SEN through extensive re-organisation.

However, this social constructionist viewpoint is considered to be a less useful position than viewing SEN as resulting from an interaction of social, physiological and psychological factors. The implications of this broader perspective are that, although mainstream schools can reorganise to meet the needs of many children with SEN, there are some children whose needs are so severe or complex that their needs cannot be met in the mainstream and therefore require specialist provision. For example, if the issue of exclusion is viewed from a psycho-social perspective, it is clear that, although a more facilitative approach to disaffection within mainstream schools should reduce rates of exclusion, there will still be some children with severe emotional and behavioural difficulties who need to have specialist help. This can best be provided in special schools or pupil referral units.

1.2.4 Curriculum

Another problem has been the confusion surrounding entitlement and the appropriateness of curricula for children with SEN. From when it was first proposed, influential people and organisations in the SEN field supported the government's intention to include children with SEN in the National Curriculum to the greatest extent possible. That all children with SEN should be entitled to have access to the same curriculum as other children was seen as being a step forward. This was in fact the case for many children, for example, those with severe visual impairment who in the past may have been denied the opportunity to take science subjects. However, for the majority of pupils with SEN, who have learning or behavioural difficulties, it has been a backward step. The National Curriculum, with its associated assessments and consequences such as league tables, has emphasised academic achievement much more than other aspects of the curriculum such as personal, social and vocational education (Dyson, 1997). Having the National Curriculum as the whole curriculum is not appropriate for these pupils and leads to many of them becoming disaffected and developing behavioural problems.

Thus, inclusion in an unsuitable curriculum directly contributes to the disaffection of many pupils, which leads them to be disruptive and eventually results in the exclusion of some of them. The priority for children with SEN, therefore, must be that they have access to curricula which are appropriate for them, not that they are fitted in to a curriculum designed for the mainstream population which may not meet their particular needs.

1.2.5 Goals

An important confusion that impinges upon issues of inclusion and exclusion concerns the goals of education. This confusion applies to all children but is particularly important for children with SEN. In recent years there has been increasing emphasis on academic achievement as the primary goal of education. Governments have focused their attention on the improvement of academic standards by various means. This has deflected attention away from the broader goals of education, such as those concerned with the development of life and social skills. This is despite the fact that there are many examples of people who have done well in adult life despite a lack of academic qualifications but there are few who are successful if they lack confidence in themselves and are unable to get on with other people.

Including pupils with SEN in mainstream schools, which are driven by the need to achieve high academic standards, results in the goals of education for many of these pupils being inappropriate. The major goal of education for the majority of children with SEN must be to produce well-adjusted and productive citizens. As noted in the Salamanca Statement on Special Needs Education:

> 'Schools should assist them to become economically active and provide them with the skills needed in everyday life, offering training in skills which respond to the social and communication demands and expectations of adult life.'

UNESCO, 1004, p. 10

Thus, for children with learning difficulties, academic achievement should be secondary to this broader goal. Likewise, the goals of education for many disaffected children who have been excluded from school should not only focus on academic achievement but also on the life and social skills necessary to become successful citizens.

1.2.6 Reality

A common confusion among many educators is that of confusing the rhetoric of full inclusion with the reality of the situation in schools. The rhetoric of inclusion suggests that it is possible to effectively educate all children with SEN in mainstream schools. However, the reality of the current situation in mainstream schools is that many teachers do not feel able or willing to cope with this scenario. In a recent review of the research on teacher perceptions of inclusion, Scruggs and Mastropieri (1996) analysed the results of twenty-eight studies published between 1958 and 1995. The major finding was that, although, on average, 65 per cent of teachers supported the general concept of inclusion, only 40 per cent believed that this is a realistic goal for most children. Fifty-three per cent of teachers reported that they were willing to teach students with disabilities and 54 per cent considered that such students could benefit from inclusion. However, only 33 per cent of teachers believed that the mainstream classroom was the best place for students with disabilities. Only 28 per cent of teachers thought that there was sufficient time available to implement inclusion and only 29 per cent considered they had sufficient expertise. An important finding was that there was no correlation between positive attitudes towards inclusion and date of publication, suggesting that teachers' views have not substantially changed over the years. Croll and Moses (2000) have recently found similar reservations among teachers in the UK.

The reality at present is also that there is minimal input on teaching pupils with SEN in initial training courses and limited in-service training available. This means that many teachers do not have the skills necessary for including pupils with a wide range of special needs in their classes (Garner, 2001). Many teachers are also concerned that there will be insufficient material and financial resources, and in particular support staff, to implement a policy of full inclusion effectively.

1.2.7 Finance

A key confusion concerns the funding of children with SEN who are included in mainstream schools. A variety of solutions to this problem have been tried by Local Education Authorities (LEAs) but there is still no agreement on what is the most satisfactory way of doing this.

There is also confusion about the relative cost of provision for SEN in mainstream or special facilities (Crowther *et al.*, 1998). At first sight, special schools and units appear expensive, so inclusion and exclusion seem to be the cheaper or easier options, in the short term. However, if the education system does not provide young people with the knowledge, skills and attitudes they need to achieve success after they leave school, the cost to society will be far greater in the long run. This cost can be seen in terms of unemployment benefits, welfare payments and the costs of the criminal justice system, as is illustrated later in this chapter. Thus, special provision for excluded children and for a small number with SEN is costly but it is likely to be much less than the later consequences of not making such provision.

1.2.8 Means and ends

The most common confusion with inclusion is concerned with whether it is a means to an end or an end in itself. Proponents of full inclusion argue that segregated SEN placement is wrong because the goal of education should be to fully include children in the community, so they ought to be included in mainstream schools.

However, inclusion in the community after leaving school is the actual end that educators are seeking. Inclusion in mainstream school may be a means to that end but is not the end itself. For some children with SEN, segregated SEN placement may be the best means to the end of eventual inclusion in the community when they leave school. Phelps and Hanley-Maxwell (1997) emphasise the need to clearly differentiate means from ends in the education of children with disabilities. Their review of the literature on transition concluded that functional curricula which integrate academic and vocational skills and supervised school work experience are the most important means of ensuring young people with disabilities obtain jobs and achieve maximum inclusion in the community as adults.

There is also confusion about the role of inclusion in schools bringing about the desired end of inclusion in society as adults. This confusion is clear in the section of the Green Paper which addresses inclusion. It states:

> 'The ultimate purpose of SEN provision is to enable young people to flourish in adult life. There are therefore strong educational, as well as social and moral, grounds for educating children with SEN with their peers. We aim to increase the level and quality of inclusion within mainstream schools, while protecting and enhancing specialist provision for those who need it.'
>
> DfEE, 1997, p. 43

This quote suggests that inclusion of children with SEN in mainstream schools will be increased in order to enable more of them to flourish in adult life. It implies that inclusion at school will promote inclusion in society as adults. However, this is clearly a naïve view since many other factors are involved, such as following an appropriate curriculum, adequate transition planning and availability of support services, which are likely to have more impact on promoting inclusion as adults than being included in mainstream schools. In addition, inclusion in mainstream schools which does not fully meet children's SEN may be counterproductive in that it could reduce the potential for full inclusion in the community as adults.

1.3   Labelling

Inclusion is regarded as preferable to some practices which are central to special education, such as the identification of SEN and the drawing up of IEPs (e.g. Ainscow, 1997) because they result in labelling children with SEN, which is seen as stigmatising them and therefore should be avoided.

However, recent research by Norwich (1999) has shown that although some labels, such as abnormality and impairment, do have negative connotations for teachers, others, such as learning difficulties and SEN do not. Norwich also makes the point that, *'If some children are identified as having SEN, there is a risk of negative labelling and stigma, while if they are* not *identified there is a risk that their individual needs will not be fully met.'*

1999, p. 180

1.4   The medical model

Inclusion is also regarded as being preferable to special education because the latter is considered as based upon a 'medical' or deficit model of intervention as opposed to focusing on student's needs and strengths. This is a confused and inaccurate view for several reasons (Bailey, 1998). Medical and psychological treatment models have influenced interventions in special education. Also, there are several different models of each of these, all of which are useful in various ways. As Bailey argues, even the pathological medical model is the preferred option in some situations. Likewise, although the behavioural and psychometric models have been the psychological models of greatest influence in special education, other disciplines within psychology such as developmental and humanistic psychology have played a significant role.

It is clear that, rather than being based on 'the medical model', special education has a much broader theoretical base and could be much more accurately described as utilising the scientific model or more specifically, a 'scientist practitioner' approach. That is, good practice in special education requires the use of appropriate interventions drawn up for various theoretical models and involving objective evaluation of effectiveness. Where the scientist practitioner model has had the least influence is with treatments such as Facilitated Communication and the Doman-Delecato Programme, which are not only ineffective but are also potentially harmful (Hornby *et al.*, 1997). This is why the movement towards full inclusion is so alarming. It is similar to these interventions in that it is neither based on sound theoretical principles nor encourages research into its effectiveness.

In itself this provides a major reason for rethinking the policy of full inclusion.

1.5   A focus on diversity

After 250 years of the development of segregated facilities for children with SEN, it is considered that although it was useful in the past twenty-five years, the policy pendulum has swung back towards the inclusion of these children in mainstream schools. The focus on inclusion has been beneficial for children with SEN in many ways, not least of which are the increased awareness of such children and understanding of their needs by teachers. Mainstream schools have also improved in their ability to cater for the diversity of pupils that they serve. However, the pendulum must not be allowed to swing so far away from segregated provision that it goes to the other extreme. Implementing a policy of inclusion of all children with SEN in their local schools would be just as problematic as returning to the days when they were all segregated. What is needed is a policy that combines a sensible balance of what has been learned from inclusion and from segregated provision.

It is therefore proposed that the best way forward for children with SEN is to replace the current obsession with 'inclusion' to a focus on 'diversity'. There are four aspects of this diversity:

◆ The first is to do with accepting and understanding the diversity of pupils' needs and strengths. That is, not only accepting that the uniqueness of each individual contributes to the richness of our experience as human beings, but also that recognising each child's unique balance of needs and strengths is the first step to effective teaching.

◆ The second aspect involves facilitating the use of a range of teaching strategies in order to provide for the diversity of learning needs. These strategies will include various approaches to differentiation of the curriculum as well as the use of procedures such as co-operative learning and peer tutoring.

◆ The third is concerned with ensuring the availability of a range of placement and service delivery options. These range from support teaching in mainstream classes, through special units in mainstream schools to separate special schools.

◆ The fourth is developing a range of curricular options in order to provide for the successful transition of all pupils to post-school life. For children with severe or profound special needs, this may mean a specialised curriculum, from the early years, designed to enable them to function as independently as possible as adults. For children with mild or moderate special needs it may simply involve a more vocationally oriented curriculum at the secondary school level.

By using the principle of diversity to guide our practice in educating children with SEN, it will be possible to maximise inclusion and minimise exclusion. The acknowledgement of diversity among children and the use of a range of teaching methods will facilitate the inclusion of as many children as possible in mainstream schools. The diversity of SEN provision and curricular options will ensure that all children, no matter how challenging or complex their needs, will receive an appropriate education.

1.6 Promoting responsible inclusion

The need to focus on diversity makes it essential to replace the rhetoric of full inclusion with the promotion of responsible inclusion. Concern about the increasing spread of inclusive practice in the USA led to a recent action research project, reported by Vaughn and Schumm (1995), which focused on the implementation of inclusive approaches in three primary schools in large urban areas. The authors worked with teachers, parents, administrators and governors at the schools over a two-year period, helping them to reorganise their provision for students with disabilities. The aims of the project were to develop more inclusive models of provision in order to meet these students' needs. The authors concluded that for inclusion to be effective, and therefore responsible rather than irresponsible and possibly damaging, inclusive practices needed to include nine components. These are:

◆ Using the extent to which students with SEN make satisfactory academic and social progress in ordinary classes as the major criteria for considering alternative interventions – as opposed to insisting on mainstream class placement regardless of the academic and social progress of students.
◆ Allowing teachers to choose whether or not they will be involved in teaching inclusive classes – as opposed to expecting all teachers, regardless of their attitudes towards inclusion or their expertise in teaching students with SEN, to teach inclusive classes.
◆ Ensuring the provision of adequate human and physical resources – as opposed to expecting reductions in the cost of provision through implementing inclusion.

◆ Encouraging schools to develop inclusive practices tailored to the needs of the students, parents and communities that they serve as well and to take into account the expertise of their own staff – as opposed to imposing inclusive models on schools without involving them in discussion.

◆ Maintaining a continuum of services including withdrawal for small group teaching and placement in special education classrooms – as opposed to viewing full inclusion as the only option.

◆ Continually monitoring and evaluating the organisation of provision in order to ensure that students' needs are being met – as opposed to sticking rigidly to one model of inclusion without ongoing evaluation to assess its effectiveness.

◆ Ensuring ongoing professional development is available to all staff who need it – as opposed to not considering teachers' need for training in order to be able to implement inclusion.

◆ Encouraging the development of alternative teaching strategies and means of adapting the curriculum in order to meet the specific needs of students with a wide range of ability – as opposed to exposing students with SEN to the same teaching and curriculum as other students.

◆ Developing an agreed philosophy and policy on inclusion which provides guidance to teachers, parents and others – as opposed to imposing a policy of inclusion on schools without the opportunity for discussion.

1.7   Focusing on transition

The focus of education programmes for students with SEN needs to be on preparation for life (McConkey, 1998), therefore, a major concern ought to be transition as well as inclusion. This is illustrated by the results of a recent study (Hornby and Kidd, 2000). The aim of the study was to investigate the outcomes of an inclusion project that had taken place in the East Riding of Yorkshire approximately ten years ago.

Twenty-nine pupils who were transferred from a special school for students with moderate learning difficulties (MLD) to mainstream schools were surveyed after just over one year in their new schools (Kidd and Hornby, 1993). It was found that a majority of the students and their parents were happy with the transfer. However, there was a noticeable difference in responses between children transferred into units within mainstream schools and those who were included in mainstream classes. Eleven out of the twelve parents whose children transferred to a school in which most of the teaching for these children was conducted in the special unit were happy with the transfer, one of the parents was neutral and none regretted the transfer. However, only eight out of the seventeen parents whose children spent most of their time in mainstream classes were happy with the transfer, five of them were neutral, and four parents regretted the transfer.

Similarly, eleven out of twelve children who transferred to the special unit were happy with the transfer, one of the children was neutral, and none regretted the transfer. However, only eleven out of the seventeen children who were taught mainly in mainstream classes were happy with the transfer, two were neutral about it, and four of them regretted the transfer.

Thus, the findings of the first survey suggested that there were generally greater levels of satisfaction, of both parents and children, for those children who were transferred to a school, which used a unit model of inclusion, rather than those who were included in mainstream classes.

A second follow-up study of these same twenty-nine young people who are now from three to nine years out of the school system has recently been conducted (Hornby and Kidd, 2000). An interview survey was carried out in order to investigate the quality of life experienced by the young people in terms of their employment status, post-school education, independence and social life.

Subjects were located by means of telephone tracing and calling in person using lists of names and addresses supplied by the LEA and the secondary schools which they last attended. Twenty-four (twelve males and twelve females) out of the twenty-nine ex-students were located giving a response rate of 83 per cent. The students had spent an average of seven years in special schools. Following the transfer they completed their education in mainstream schools, spending an average of three years there. The subjects left school between 1991 and 1997 and were aged between 18 and 25 years (mean 22 years) at the time of the study in January 2000.

At the time of the survey seventeen out of the twenty-four ex-students were unemployed. One was at home with her children aged two and three years. Two were attending Resource Centres that provided sheltered employment. One was working part-time at a supermarket and receiving the severe disability allowance. Three were working full-time: one on a pig farm, another as a care assistant in a residential home and the other as a packer in a pill factory. A further five ex-students had worked in at least one job since leaving school but were currently unemployed. In addition, two of the young men without regular jobs reported that they had found alternative ways of earning money. One kept ferrets and used them to catch rabbits, which he then sold to a local butcher. The other bought old bicycles, fixed them up and sold them to various people.

Of grave concern is that sixteen of the twenty-four young people were reported to be on severe disability allowance. Seventeen of them lived with their parents, one lived with her sister, one lived with her partner and two lived alone in rented flats. Two were in residential care and one was held in a psychiatric unit.

None of the subjects were married. None owned a car or motorcycle or had obtained their driving licence, although two were currently taking driving lessons. Three had convictions for various offences. Eleven subjects reported having no friends, six having one friend, four having two or three friends and three having more than three friends. Seventeen subjects reported their leisure activities to be watching TV or videos, thirteen listening to music, six going to the pub, five computer games, five swimming, four bike riding, three shopping, three attending youth clubs and two reading.

When asked to comment on the transfer from special to mainstream school for their final years of schooling, fifteen rated it as helpful, while nine rated it as unhelpful. When these ratings were analysed separately for subjects who had been included in mainstream classes and those who had been included in a unit within a mainstream school, a clear pattern emerged. Eleven of the twelve subjects who had been included in units viewed the transfer positively while this was the case for only three out of the twelve subjects who had been included in mainstream classes.

The greater satisfaction of ex-unit pupils was borne out by many of their spontaneous comments during the interviews. For example, six subjects mentioned that they had been bullied in their mainstream schools whereas only one of the ex-unit subjects mentioned this. In addition to the greater consumer satisfaction with the unit model of inclusion, these findings highlight the low level of inclusion in their community which these young people have achieved as adults. It appears that, while strenuous efforts were made to ensure that these young people experienced inclusion for their last few years of schooling, insufficient attention was paid to facilitating their transition from school to adult life. From the interviews it appears that what was missing from their secondary school programmes were the following:

◆ functional curricula to teach them the skills they needed;
◆ comprehensive, well-supervised work experience schemes;
◆ effective transition planning which involved parents and the young people;
◆ support networks of agencies to provide guidance to parents and the young people themselves after they left school.

These aspects need to be paid greater attention in the future as part of comprehensive frameworks for promoting successful transition (McGinty and Fish, 1992). The elements of such frameworks have been identified by Phelps and Hanley-Maxwell (1997) and are summarised below:

◆ programme administration: including leadership, resources, staff development and evaluation procedures;
◆ curriculum: including individualised transition plans, functional academic and vocational training, suitable settings and instructional methods such as co-operative learning;
◆ support services: including learning support, assessment of interests and abilities and vocational guidance;
◆ communication networks: including involvement of students, parents, teachers and other professionals in transition planning, vocational preparation and inter-agency collaboration;
◆ follow-up: including work experience opportunities, job placement services and agencies able to provide ongoing support and guidance.

1.8 A focus on outcome research

A key component in achieving quality education for children with SEN is evaluation of programme effectiveness. McConkey has expressed dismay over the lack of research in this area. He says: '*At a minimum, we need to follow up the career paths of young people graduating from special education and trace correlates between outcomes and inputs*'. There is a long history of follow-up studies of people with disabilities in the UK. Tizard (1958) describes studies dating back to the 1920s. In the USA there is an ongoing national longitudinal study of outcomes for youth with disabilities (Blackorby and Wagner, 1996). Recent follow-up studies of young people with disabilities have also been conducted in Australia (Riches *et al.*, 1996). But there is a dearth of such follow-up or outcome

McConkey, 1998, p. 59

research that has been carried out in the UK. Because of the increase in the number of inclusion projects being put in place in the UK and because of the disappointing outcomes of the follow-up study reported earlier, it seems more important now than ever that outcome research is widely conducted.

Martin (1994, quoted in Crockett and Kauffman, 1999) who has been involved in drafting US legislation on children with disabilities from PL 94–142 onwards has stated: *'New programs designed to include all children with disabilities in regular classes should be carefully tested and replicated widely only when they are demonstrated to work'.*

Crockett and Kauffman, 1000, p. 22

Tizard (1978) in his article on research needed in the field of special education suggested that the four criteria for integration stipulated in the Warnock Report (DES, 1978) provide a useful framework for designing evaluations of integration projects. Feedback from these evaluations would provide evidence regarding the effectiveness of inclusion and thereby facilitate the improvement of future practice. This is a crucial need in the field of special needs education in the UK.

1.9 Conclusion

The focus of attention in special needs education needs to shift from promoting full inclusion to implementing responsible inclusion. This requires clarification of the major confusions surrounding inclusion and a commitment to a policy of working with a diversity of pupils, methods and settings. In order to improve the quality of the lives of young people with SEN, much more attention needs to be paid to their transition from school to adult life and to the evaluation of programmes through outcome research.

References

Ainscow, M. 'Towards inclusive schooling', *British Journal of Special Education* 24 (1), 1997, pp. 3–6.

Bailey, J. 'Medical and psychological models in special needs education', in *Theorising Special Education*, C. Clark, A. Dyson and A. Millward (eds), London, Routledge, 1998.

Blackorby, J. and Wagner, M. 'Longitudinal postschool outcomes of youth with disabilities: findings from the National Longitudinal Transition Study', *Exceptional Children*, 62 (5), 1996, pp. 399–413.

Bronfenbrenner, U. *The Ecology of Human Development*, Cambridge, MA, Harvard University Press, 1979.

Centre for the Studies of Inclusive Education *The Inclusion Charter*, Bristol, CSIE, 1989.

Crockett, J.B. and Kauffman, J.M. *The Least Restrictive Environment: Its Origins and Interpretations in Special Education*, Mahwah, NJ, Lawrence Erlbaum, 1999.

Croll, P. and Moses, D. 'Ideologies and utopias: educational professionals' view of inclusion', *European Journal of Special Needs Education*, 15 (1), 2000, pp. 1–12.

Crowther, D., Dyson, A., Elliott, J. and Millward, A. *Costs and Outcomes for Pupils with Moderate Learning Difficulties (MLD) in Special and Mainstream Schools*, London, DfEE, 1998.

Department for Education and Science *Special Educational Needs: Report of the Committee of Enquiry into the Education of Handicapped Children and Young People*, London, HMSO, 1978.

Department for Education and Employment *Excellence for All Children: Meeting Special Educational Needs*, London, DfEE, 1997.

Department for Education and Employment *Meeting Special Educational Needs: A Programme for Action*, Sudbury, DfEE, 1998.

Dyson, A. 'Social and educational disadvantage: reconnecting special needs education', *British Journal of Special Education*, 24 (4), 1997, pp. 152–7.

Garner, P. 'Goodbye Mr Chips', Chapter 4 in this volume, 2001.

Hornby, G. 'Inclusion or delusion: can one size fit all?', *Support for Learning* 14 (4), 1999, pp. 152–7.

Hornby, G., Atkinson, M. and Howard, J. *Controversial Issues in Special Education*, London, David Fulton Publishers, 1997.

Hornby, G. and Kidd, R. 'Transfer from special to mainstream: ten years later', *British Journal of Special Education* 28 (1), 2001, pp. 10–17.

Kauffman, J.M. 'Foreword' in *The Ethics of Special Education*, K.R. Howe and O.B. Miramontes, New York, Teachers College Press, 1992, pp. xi–xvii.

Kidd, R. and Hornby, G. 'Transfer from special to mainstream', *British Journal of Special Education* 20 (1), 1993, pp. 17–19.

McConkey, R. 'Education for life?', *British Journal of Special Education* 25 (2), 1998, pp. 55–9.

McGinty, J. and Fish, J. *Learning Support for Young People in Transition*, Milton Keynes, Open University Press, 1992.

Lindsay, G. 'Values, rights and dilemmas', *British Journal of Special Education* 24 (2), 1997, pp. 55–9.

Norwich, B. 'The connotation of special education labels for professionals in the field', *British Journal of Special Education* 26 (4), 1999, pp. 179–83.

O'Brien, T. 'The Millennium Curriculum: confronting the issues and proposing solutions', *Support for Learning* 13 (4), 1998, pp. 147–52.

Phelps, L.A. and Hanley-Maxwell, C.H. 'School to work transitions for youth with disabilities: a review of outcomes and practices', *Review of Educational Research* 67 (2), 1997, pp. 197–226.

Riches, V.C., Parmenter, T.R. and Robertson, G. *Youth with Disabilities in Transition from School to Community*, Sydney: Macquarie University, 1996.

Scruggs, T.E. and Mastropieri, M.A. 'Teacher perceptions of mainstreaming/inclusion, 1958–1995: a research synthesis', *Exceptional Children*, 63 (1), 1996, pp. 59–74.

Tizard, J. 'Longitudinal and follow-up studies', in *Mental Deficiency: The Changing Outlook*, A.M. Clarke and A.D.B. Clarke (eds), New York, Free Press, 1958.

Tizard, J. 'Research in special education', *Special Education: Forward Trends* 5 (3), 1978, pp. 23–6.

Thomson, J.J. *The Realm of Rights*, Cambridge, MA, Harvard University Press, 1990.

UNESCO *The Salamanca Statement and Framework for Action on Special Needs Education*, New York, UNESCO, 1994.

Vaughn, S. and Schumm, J.S. 'Responsible inclusion for students with learning disabilities', *Journal of Learning Disabilities* 28 (5), 1995, pp. 264–70.

Janet Tod

> '*The introduction of statutory funding, curricular and assessment frameworks brings this child-centred education to a crisis, since the organising principle of management becomes one of accountability to structures hierarchically far removed from the immediate and daily needs of any child (although they are surely intended to guarantee the meeting of such needs).*'

Clough, 1999

Clough was referring to recent developments in UK special education...and will it be the same with inclusion?

This chapter seeks to view inclusion from the perspective of the individual. It is hoped that this may help to address the credibility gap that currently exists between the ideology and implementation of inclusion within educational settings. By acknowledging that the concerns of individual teachers, pupils and parents have credence, it is hoped that these important stakeholders will be afforded entry into a debate from which they have been largely excluded. Policy development for educational inclusion has to date been a top-down process which has so far denied individual stakeholders and participants the opportunity for ownership and involvement. While there are no easy answers to achieving the complexity of varying levels of inclusion, it is clear that a concern for individual rights within educational settings should not be eclipsed by an ideological commitment to inclusion.

2.1 Inclusion and emergent concerns for individual teachers

The current agenda for coping with diversity in education (DfEE, 1998) has been agreed on the basis of face validity and the adoption of an appropriate moral and social stance. The requirement that the values of equity and inclusion should be realised in contexts where the curriculum has been determined (DfEE/QCA, 1999) and academic outcomes prescribed has fuelled debate among individuals involved in the field of special education. In essence, debates are centred upon addressing the credibility gap that exists between the rhetoric and reality of inclusive education (Clark *et al.*, 1999). Two consistently emerging areas for debate concern the 'right' and 'might' of inclusive education.

The 'might' (politically led) tends to focus on the educational *context* in which inclusive practices are intended to flourish. There is a perceived tension between the development of inclusive practices and the continuation of national academic attainment targets for prescribed percentages of the population. In addition, some apparent paradoxes in provision and policy continue to be supported by the government. These include selective education based on academic ability for some; exclusion from the mainstream classroom based on behaviour for others; the continued use of the term 'special educational needs' and individual education plans (IEPs) and the option for parental choice of special school placement. While some hold dear the view that segregation and exclusion are socially constructed and can therefore logically be deconstructed to promote full inclusion, others are of the opinion that this reasoning is flawed (Fuchs and Fuchs, 1994; Zigmoid and Baker, 1996). This leaves teachers with at least two challenges:

1. They have to balance their role in promoting educational inclusion and meeting national attainment targets.

2. They are required to contribute to the deconstruction of segregation and exclusion within their setting on the basis of a belief that this is the solution to tackling inequalities and social exclusion within education.

In struggling to meet these expectations teachers not only have to bear the burden of trying to make inclusion work but risk experiencing failure if the predicted outcomes of inclusion fail to materialise.

The 'right' of the inclusion debate centres around philosophical issues concerning a human rights agenda and a belief that meeting individual children's needs overrides an ideological commitment to inclusion concerns (Croll and Moses, 2000). As stated by the Department for Education:

'Where pupils do have special educational needs there are strong educational, social and moral grounds for their education in mainstream schools. Our policy for schools will be consistent with our commitment to rights for disabled people more generally. But we must always put the needs of the child first and for some children specialist, and perhaps residential, provision will be required, at least for a time. This is compatible with the principle of inclusive education.'

DfEE, 1999 p. 34

This concern about individual rights has also triggered debate about whether certain individuals can arguably be given exemption from being educated in inclusive local schools on grounds which are similar to those given in the Warnock Report (DES, 1978). This justified a continued role for special schools, but in this instance in the context of integration, including the following:

◆ difficulties and differences experienced by some individuals are such that any placement in mainstream is likely to be purely locational and tokenistic to inclusion, e.g. those with profound, multiple and complex learning difficulties; those with severe social communication difficulties; those considered to need combined educational and care placement;
◆ the behaviour of the individual concerned interferes with inclusion for others;
◆ the individual concerned has opted not to be included. For example, some individuals with sensory difficulties may prefer to be schooled in a setting which allows sign language to be the predominant form of communication (Corker, 1998). Individuals who experience considerable emotional difficulties may be unable to partake in the relationships needed to effect inclusion and may 'opt out' by refusing to co-operate.

A consideration of 'individual right' within inclusive educational contexts naturally leads to consideration of choice and inclusion (Riddell, 2000). While the government's position on choice is clear, as outlined by Schools Minister Jacqui Smith in a written answer to the House of Commons:

> *'Where parents want a mainstream setting for their child our policy is to try to provide it. Equally, when parents want a specialist setting for their child it is important that their wishes are respected ...We are advocating inclusion by choice and have underlined that there remains a continuing and vital role for special schools.'*

Smith, 1 February 2000

It remains a matter for debate whether giving such choice will undermine the inclusion movement by allowing individuals, their parents/guardians, and teachers the option to exclude themselves from community-based inclusive schools. Riddell suggests that support for individual choice within inclusion is influenced by the purpose behind the policy:

> *'the principles of integration and choice are treated very differently in official policy documents and the writing of the disability movement ... within official discourse ... wishes of parents are seen to take*

2000, p. 109

priority over the desire to run the school on integrated lines ... the disability movement has a different set of priorities based on the pursuit of rights for disabled people ... For the disability movement, the principle of inclusion is generally prioritised over that of choice.'

Interestingly, those at the forefront of debate, whose views are available in the public domain, are educational researchers, policy-makers, and academics. Much less is known about the views of recipients and deliverers of inclusive education – namely, pupils, their parents and teachers.

As a consequence of the speed and nature of government control of education, teachers have become conditioned to accepting imposed constraints to inclusion knowing that their voices will be largely unheard, and that some pupils and institutions will become beneficiaries of policy while others will be victims of that same policy. They will come to acknowledge the positive outcomes of imposed policy and adjust their attitudes accordingly, while reflecting upon the personal and professional costs of this rapid cycle of policy implementation. Responses from practitioners tend to be concerned with the feasibility of implementation ('how?'), educational researchers with the rational and rigour ('why?'), and LEAs, with cost, accountability and evaluation ('what?'). While debate and enquiry continue into the rationale and feasibility of educational inclusion, it has to be accepted that increased inclusive practices have been prescribed and will be subjected to external monitoring (OfSTED, 2000). Failure to meet OfSTED requirements for inclusion are likely to be attributed to implementation defects (usually teachers) and will be followed by the distribution of additional guidance documents which will probably include selected vignettes of good practice developed by teachers and schools during their 'discovery learning' period of implementation. Subsequent legislation will serve to modify original policy requirements on inclusion leaving the way forward for another politically generated educational initiative to take centre stage.

And so, what is the problem? Other educational initiates for diversity have come and gone – teachers have learned to cope, schools to adapt and parents to accept. What is so special about inclusion? Why is it that a real commitment to inclusion is so important? Perhaps it is because the principles behind inclusion transcend those that are housed within education and employment. There is no quick fix, no defined end point, no abandonment if it fails, no rigging of outcomes for individuals – the need to foster inclusion is a *consequence* of our developing and changing society and as such there is no turning back. That is why the involvement of primary stakeholders in debate and practice is essential if individuals are to avoid conscription to educational changes that are based on ideology, hope, and rhetoric. If progress is to be made with the development of inclusion there is a need to start with the anticipated *outcomes* of inclusion for individuals and translate them into setting conditions. That is, start with empowered individuals, a learning society, diversity in starting points and responses, collaborative and creative practices, flexible and appropriate outcomes, and ongoing dynamic responsive and self-critical activity. Plus an acceptance that uncertainty is as central to the development of society as is the power of human adaptation to change. Within SEN education circles there is support for the ideal of educational inclusion coupled with concerns about putting inclusion into practice (Wedell, 2000). It is crucial that this commitment to inclusion which practitioners undoubtedly feel is channelled into the development of appropriate provision for individuals.

For this to happen there is a need to redress the balance between stakeholder influence in the inclusion process. Inclusion as a philosophical ideal has been adopted, interpreted and reconstructed by those involved in education. As far as teachers are concerned, the dominant perspective is the one provided by the government (DfEE, 1998; DfEE/QCA, 1999) which will be interpreted by Local Education Authorities (LEAs) and communicated to their schools. The 'index of inclusion' (CSIE, 2000b) designed to support the development of inclusion in schools, has been endorsed by the DfEE and distributed to all schools. It guides schools into taking ownership of their response to given inclusionist ideals. It is at this point that individuals involved in school development need to model the principles of inclusion and collaboratively make decisions about how best to put inclusion into practice in their own setting. Inclusion might be regarded as an absolute concept for some policy-makers but for individuals it is a relative concept linked to the social context of time and place. Schools will be judged on their ability to supply evidence of an increase in inclusive practices and although the consensus of change may enable comparisons between schools, the impact of a change in policy on individual pupils will be more difficult to gauge. If the child 'with special educational needs' is to be re-designated as the 'included pupil', it is important that he/she should be a beneficiary of this change. For this to happen, the individual's response to inclusive policies must not be hidden in a school statistic but given due consideration in its own right.

Inclusion for individuals occurs at different levels of school experience and planning. Inclusion will be a developmental process in schools. Each level of inclusion may be evaluated separately with different outcomes At the whole school policy level an individual might be deemed to be included if 'inclusive policies are in place' but the individual concerned may not be experiencing the anticipated effect of being included (Tod, 1999). It is for this reason that schools need to develop policies and practices that enable inclusion to occur and also to examine whether individuals have been enabled by that process. If enabling educational inclusion is to become a reality for individuals, then it is necessary for schools to consider inclusion initiatives designed for collective purposes (inclusive schools, inclusive communities, inclusive society) from the viewpoint of the individual.

Table 2.1 represents key issues that have been raised in the literature and in discussion with teachers attending in-service training (INSET) courses.

Areas of debate arising from current policy	Individual perspective and concerns	Examples given by teachers
Inclusive policy for education has been informed from a human rights agenda – inclusion is morally necessitated. The aim is to develop a society in which all learners are valued and participant members.	In planning for inclusion which takes priority – the needs of the group or the needs of the individual? If individual needs take priority and some individuals are perceived to need 'different' education (e.g. individuals with severe sensory or emotional difficulties), does this happen at the cost of developing an inclusive society? – is the aim for an inclusion society or a less exclusionary society?	Given that the Literacy Hour is designed with zero exclusion in mind but also has as an aim to 'increase time spend actively learning literacy' is it justifiable to: a) exclude an individual pupil who is persistently disturbing the class from participating in the hour? b) consider educating some pupils with considerable access and participation difficulties in a different setting so that their chances of learning literacy are increased?
Choice v/s inclusion	Does the notion of a 'community school' restrict, or conflict with, the notion of parental choice	How should I react to a parent who wants her child to go to a residential special school on the grounds that he will have a 24-hour curriculum which will give him more time learning and more chance of mixing socially with his peers?

Areas of debate arising from current policy	Individual perspective and concerns	Examples given by teachers
Theoretical models on which practice is based: the dominant model for inclusion in the UK is the social model of disability which is concerned with 'reducing barriers' to learning and social participation.	Is the adoption of a sociological model of disability a necessary or sufficient condition to fully meet the needs of individual pupils? For many children difficulties in learning arise from biological and psychological factors. If social deconstruction and reconstruction of disability could be achieved via initiatives for inclusion, would equity for individuals be achieved? Is inclusion for individuals about removing barriers *and* building bridges?	I have a pupil in my class who has chosen to exclude himself from learning and social activities. In this case, when a pupil has a long history of emotional and behavioural problems, is it possible that his psychological problems are preventing him from taking advantage of what we feel is a more inclusive school than many?
Are the social and academic aims of inclusive education of equal importance as is suggested by the two expressed aims of Curriculum 2000?	Evidence from the literature suggests that for many individuals there are social benefits to being placed in mainstream settings – the belief that inclusive education is the best way of improving attainment for individuals has yet to be validated by research.	We have a pupil with Asperger's Syndrome who is unable to benefit from the interactive teaching within the Literacy Hour because he does not share the perspectives of his peers. He is very bright and an excellent reader – we feel that he experiences such difficulties in social situations that at times this interferes with his learning and so there is a justification for not trying to tackle academic and social aspects of learning at the same time.
Should individuals be supported to learn or should learning support be integral to school practice for all pupils?	What is the purpose of learning support for individual pupils? If LSAs are to become less involved with individuals, does this reduce the 'different' or 'otherwise extra' provision they need and the close monitoring of their responses to class teaching?	In our school the LSAs take responsibility for individual monitoring of pupil responses to their IEP. I can see that some pupils can become dependent on individual LSA support but that is monitored via the IEP targets which describe the conditions under which the target is achieved. Dependency on the LSA can occur but teacher attention to one individual is necessarily limited by class size – in a class of 30 that works out to approx. 8 minutes per individual per day

Areas of debate arising from current policy	Individual perspective and concerns	Examples given by teachers
Outcomes: long or short term?	As the long-term aim of inclusion is to promote equity and social participation, is it reasonable to suggest that any one individual could achieve those long-term aims via a variety of educational experiences? These could include a period of special school placement e.g. in a unit where specialist provision is available for EBD, so that the pupil could, in time, be able to respond to the opportunities offered by mainstream inclusive setting.	We have a pupil in our school who has experienced disrupted home placements and has been 'in and out of care'. Given the poor long-term outcomes for looked after children, we feel that he needs time in a small group specialist setting and some one-to-one relationship experience which he has been so far denied. If he can't relate on an individual level, how can he function effectively in a group?
Specialist or mainstream provision	Is teaching for diversity any more than 'good' teaching? If all teachers adopted inclusive teaching strategies would that be sufficient to meet individual pupil needs?	I have a pupil with a language difficulty who has been assessed as needing 'different and extra' provision via her IEP. None of our teachers meet the TTA specialist standards for specialist teaching of such pupils and we have found that good teaching as described by Ainscow (2000) does not make up for lack of specialism in this area.
Equity through valuing diversity or 'normalisation'?	Should we seek to assess and value different outcomes for individual pupils or try to encourage pupils towards NLS, NNS outcomes irrespective of time taken?	I have a pupil in my class for whom the pace and content of the NLS are simply out of his reach. We have designed targets based on QCA additional targets but this seems to be just a way of saying that the pupil shares the curriculum. The targets might be relevant for the government but not for the pupil.

2.2 From reasoning on inclusion to reality for the individual

Inclusion has the ingredients needed to write the recipe for an inclusive educational diet that should promote equity and participation for learners. It has a philosophy, a supporting theoretical stance, a critical stance on current practice, and suggestions for change. Prescription and evaluation of outcomes have yet to be explicitly tackled on the grounds that any 'negative' outcomes would reflect a flaw in implementation of a principle that is beyond scrutiny (Clark *et al.*, 1998). So will this inclusive diet be sufficient to nourish individual learners?

2.2.1 Philosophy

> *'Regular schools with an inclusive orientation are the most effective way of combating discriminatory attitudes, creating welcoming communities, building on an inclusive society and achieving education for all; moreover they provide an effective education to the majority of children and improve the efficiency and ultimately the cost effectiveness of the entire education system.'*
>
> CSIE, 1995, p. 8

This refers to the Salamanca Statement (UNESCO, 1994) description of an inclusive orientation where all children are to be accommodated in ordinary schools regardless of physical, intellectual, social, emotional, linguistic or other conditions. At least two problems arise from this philosophy for individuals:

> *'So we might wonder whether an inclusive philosophy is not also naïve, but also dishonest, because it assumes what it seeks to establish; that is, inclusion is morally necessitated and structurally indicated: get the structures right, one might say and humanity will follow. However, it cannot be assumed that inclusion is a simple "given" of natural life, a necessary property of consciousness or culture.'*
>
> Clough, 1999

Individuals in their language development and early social behaviour do not seek to engage and participate in 'society'. They actively seek to reduce complexity and personalise their world by identifying similarities and differences and opting to relate to those individuals with whom they identify similarities. This is presumably an adaptive mechanism that serves to reinforce the strengths inherent in close relationships (family, peers, etc.). The notion of an inclusive society has yet to be translated for individuals within that society. Belonging may be evidenced by passport documentation but only experienced and realised at a level at which relationships are personalised such as family and friendships. Achievement is often fuelled by competition and the philosophy of inclusion needs to battle with the theory of 'survival of the fittest' if it is to impact on all individuals.

Second, if discrimination and marginalisation of certain groups of individuals on the basis of disability, race or gender are presumed to be socially engineered, then it follows that deconstruction and reconstruction at the macro level (e.g. institutional, community) will be sufficient to effect changes at the micro (e.g. small group, peer and individual) level. While there is considerable face validity in this notion and knowledge that changes at the macro level can be achieved by government intervention, it does not tackle the issue that every individual will react to 'inclusion' in different ways. Changes in individual human behaviour cannot be assured by the prescription and engineering inherent in imposed policy changes. Statistics may indicate an 'average' change but inclusion is about relationships. *'It is concerned with the careful fostering of a mutually sustaining relationship between local centres of learning and all members of their surrounding communities.'*

Booth, 2000

The acknowledgement that inclusion is about relationships is an important one. It supports notions of process, complexity, vulnerability, resilience, uncertainty and change. It recognises that a pre-targeted, measurable, fixed trajectory model is inappropriate. It raises questions concerning models, hinting that an ecosystemic model may be more appropriate for planning and assessment purposes (Cooper and Upton, 1990). It supports beliefs by practitioners that some individuals such as those who have not developed a stable relationship with anyone as a consequence of early rearing experiences will not be able to be beneficiaries of placement in the complex and impersonal social world of even the most inclusive school. Such individuals may well need individual, small group provision before they are grouped with their peers in their community school. Individuals need to develop characteristics that will enable them to respond to the opportunities inherent in inclusion. Interestingly, one of the most effective forms of inclusive learning can be seen during the early development of language within the small group setting of the family or equivalent unit. The caretaker/parent does not regard the newborn infant as an individual with a learning difficulty. The impetus for action appears to be the development of social communication within a reciprocal relationship. This relationship mirrors much of what is valued in inclusive learning: the enabling framework, the creation of opportunities to learn, the value placed on both affective and intellectual development, the value given to the infant's struggle to communicate, the celebration when communication is achieved, the empowering of the infant, shared attention and active engagement, and above all close monitoring and subsequent adjustment by the parent/caregiver. Once this type of relationship is established, the caretaker/parent changes aspects of the relationship to prepare the infant to function in the wider context of siblings, family, peers, playgroup and school (Tod and Blamires, 1998). There is a reduction in total acceptance, increased control, instruction as to social conventions and required learning and behavioural outcomes. Close monitoring continues. This stage of development of the one to one relationship that is gradually extended appears to be central to the development of learning and social behaviour in the wider less personalised context. Sure Start programmes are based on this premise and yet it is interesting that for most young socially deprived children early 'group' placement is often the strategy of choice. It appears that recovery rate from early damaged relationships is slow and many pupils seek individual attention in schools as a consequence. An inclusion programme which does not give credence to the value of close individual monitoring, planning for some individual support, and flexibility of strategy to enhance individual learning may have ignored the important difference between those individuals who cannot and/or will not be responsive to inclusion (O'Brien, 2001). The 'individual' appears to have been largely forgotten in the planning of the inclusion process.

In both the learning of language and the development of social relationships humans reduce complexity by sorting for similarities and differences and creating 'constructs' to facilitate communication. Placed in an impersonal and large school setting most pupils reduce important relationships to one individual ('best friend') or a small group ('my gang'). This allows for the development of a 'personal/belonging' dimension which enables individuals to function in the larger setting. We know very little about how individual responses to inclusion will develop and more information is needed regarding how to enable individuals to develop and sustain relationships with peers – particularly if they have failed or have been prevented from establishing relationships within their own family. Do peer relationships provide a needed break from academic 'learning', do they contribute to academic learning, how do they influence emotional development? We know a great deal about the development and consequences of mother–infant relationships and far less about peer relationships.

How much do we know about the impact on learning of an individual's relationship with their community? Few individuals are actively involved in the design and sustenance of community activity. Some individuals have a parasitic relationship using the facilities to meet individual, often short-term, needs with little or no commitment or involvement. Others use the community to engineer changes within that community either for a self-centred or altruistic motive.

How do levels of relationship impact upon individuals? If personal relationships fail, do we move outwards to peers, then to activities such as clubs and cultures, then move out altogether and live on the streets in a place well away from home and community? Or if personal relationships are a success, does that give us confidence to move out into the wider social context? We cannot afford to assume that creating the conditions for inclusion, or reducing the boundaries between class, race, gender, or disability will suffice to reduce the chances that individuals will choose to exclude themselves from school and some cultural groupings. Indeed, it has been noted by one of the authors of the index for inclusion (Ainscow, 2000) 'that the indices of inclusion are about facilitating participation rather than participation *per se*'.

2.3   Theory: social modelling of inclusion

While there is little doubt that a social modelling perspective has much to offer inclusion in terms of setting appropriate contexts in which inclusive practices can develop, the key question is whether this model *alone* is sufficient to assure individual rights to a quality education. There remain concerns about the simplistic solutions offered within this approach, e.g. the notion that changing structures, curriculum and attitudes is sufficient to ensure that quality individual provision will follow. This model seeks validation via selective critiques of psychological and biological perspectives on disability. As a consequence, progress made during the history of special education has been dismissed rather than built upon. The individual is not a predictable recipient of social change but develops unique responses that are also influenced by biological and psychological factors. An individual with social communication difficulties is likely to be less responsive to the inclusive context, described by Ainscow, which *'involves the creation of a problem solving culture including learning how to use one another's experiences and resources in order to devise better ways of overcoming barriers to learning'*, than is a pupil with physical disabilities. The social modelling of inclusion advocates broadening the range of individuals who experience barriers to learning to include all learners. This broadening, which presumably increases the range of diversity, contrasts with the simplicity of using one model to address all individual differences and difficulties. The history of special education reflects that it is naïve to assume that there is one model which can serve to enable prediction and

Ainscow, 2000

control of human behaviour in such a way that change in the desired direction can be achieved for all individuals.

2.4   Methodology

Those advocating the adoption of a social model of inclusion employ research methodologies which include comparative case studies, action research, and discourse analysis (Blamires, 2001). The emphasis is on research that examines process not outcomes. Clark *et al.*, when referring to Lingard 1966 state:

> *'However, at no point do they attempt to derive principles of equity and inclusion from their empirical investigations. The question is not whether such principles actually work for the children or whether it is possible for schools to realise them; rather it is how far and in what ways schools are successful in realising principles that are not susceptible to empirical investigation ... the charge that it [research] is based on ideal types and idealised models rather than the realities of schools is not altogether without foundation.'*

Clark *et al.*, 1999

As a consequence of the methodology used, it has been strongly suggested that special school placement offers a restricted curriculum, is not cost-effective, and is, by existence, an exclusionary force within education. The use of learning support assistants (LSAs) for individual pupils is also a causal factor in developing dependency and reducing opportunities for social inclusion. The use of outside expertise is also queried on the grounds that diversity is itself a resource and *'in most schools the expertise needed to teach all pupils effectively is usually available amongst the teaching staff'*. The problem with the methodology used is the lack of rigour that results in researcher bias and unacceptable generalisation of findings. Of course, some special schools have, in the past, delivered a narrow curriculum which has resulted in barriers to entitlement for some learners. Since 1988, however, most special schools have adopted the National Curriculum and subsequent modifications and additions including the National Literacy and Numeracy strategies. The case against special schools and special provision is far from proven due mainly to the fact that individual learner response differs (Hornby, 2001). Similarly, LSA support may not foster inclusive learning and relationships but that is not a truism for all LSA support (Mencap, 1999). Specialist expertise may not always prove useful to teachers but in many cases it is welcomed and valued (Croll and Moses, 2000). It would appear to be a retrograde step, in the history of

Ainscow, 2000

educational research, to base a significant change in educational provision on research which has largely abandoned notions of reliability and validity and accepts that generalisation from case study research is allowable simply because inclusion does not have to be justified.

2.5   Implementation

Policy development for inclusion has transposed utopian ideals for an inclusive learning society onto a context in which the curriculum content and outcomes are prescribed for the majority but not all learners. The adoption of a social model has resulted in advice for teachers that includes:

◆ interactive teaching techniques;
◆ the use of 'inclusive' questioning approaches;
◆ collaborative problem-solving (staff and pupils);
◆ supported learning;
◆ planning in action;
◆ formative assessment.

The suggestion seems to be that 'good teaching' will suffice to address the needs of diverse learners in a system where the timely meeting of set targets is prescribed. It is little wonder that teachers and parents have reservations about the reality behind the rhetoric of inclusion.

2.6   Conclusion

Inclusion is about human rights, equity and participation. While there is consensus that continued developments in special education should support these ideals, there remains doubt about the philosophy, theory and practice behind current initiatives for inclusive education. Of particular concern is the fact that educational policy has been directed towards achieving collective results ('an inclusive society') and 'school' indicators. Although diversity is a key theme of inclusion, it seems paradoxical that individual differences and indeed the individual within the inclusion process have received limited attention. Given that diversity should be valued and used as a resource, it would seem timely that individual perspectives on inclusion are given their due regard. Integration has been criticised for trying to fit the individual to the school. Inclusion runs the risk of fitting the individual to a belief based on human rights. It is possible that a right to an appropriate education which will enable individuals both to increase and make choices about how to live their lives could be jeopardised in the process.

References

Ainscow, M. 'The next step in special education: supporting the development of inclusive practices', *British Journal of Special Education* 27 (2), 2000, pp. 76–80.

Blamires, M. 'Is a social model sufficient to enable inclusive educational practice?', Chapter 7 in this volume, 2001.

Booth, T. 'Inclusion and exclusion policy in England: who controls the agenda?', in *Inclusive Education: Policy, Contexts and Comparative Perspectives*, F. Armstrong, D. Armstrong and L. Barton (eds), London, David Fulton Publishers, 2000.

Centre for Studies in Inclusive Education *International Perspectives on Inclusion*, Bristol, CSIE, 1995.

Centre for Studies in Inclusive Education *The Right to Belong to the Mainstream*, Bristol, CSIE, 2000a.

Centre for Studies in Inclusive Education *Index for Inclusion*, Bristol, CSIE, 2000b.

Clark, C., Dyson, A. and Millward, A. 'Theorising special education – time to move on?', in *Theorising Special Education,* C. Clark, A. Dyson and A. Millward, London, Routledge, 1998.

Clough, P. 'Exclusive tendencies: concepts, consciousness and curriculum in the project of inclusion', *International Journal of Inclusive Education* 3 (1), 1999, pp. 63–73.

Cooper, P. and Upton, G. 'An ecosystemic approach to emotional and behavioural difficulties in schools', *Educational Psychology*, 10 (4), 1990, pp. 301–21.

Corker, M. 'Disability discourse in a post-modern world', in *The Disability Reader*, T. Shakspeare (ed.), London, Cassell, 1998.

Croll, P. and Moses, D. 'Ideologies and utopias: educational professionals' view of inclusion', *European Journal of Special Needs Education*, 15 (1), 2000, pp. 1–12.

Department for Education and Employment *Excellence for All Children: Meeting Special Educational Needs*, London, HMSO, 1997.

Department for Education and Employment *Meeting Special Educational Needs: A Programme of Action*, Sudbury, DfEE, 1998.

Department for Education and Employment and the Qualifications and Curriculum Authority *The National Curriculum*, London, DfEE, 1999.

Department of Education and Science *Special Educational Needs: Report of the Committee of Enquiry into the Education of Handicapped Children and Young People*, London, HMSO, 1978.

Fuchs, D. and Fuchs. L. 'Inclusive School Movement and the radicalisation of special education reform', *Exceptional Children*, 60 (4), 1994, pp. 294–309.

Hornby, G. 'Promoting responsible inclusion: quality education for all', Chapter 1 in this volume, 2001.

Lingard, T. 'Why our theoretical models of integration are inhibiting effective integration', *Emotional and Behavioural Difficulties* 1 (2), 1966, pp. 39–45.

Mencap *On a Wing and a Prayer: Inclusion and Children with Severe Learning Difficulties*, London, Mencap, 1999.

O'Brien, T. 'Learning from the hard cases', Chapter 3 in this volume, 2001.

Office for Standards in Education *Educational Inclusion and School Inspection*, London, HMSO, 2000.

Riddell, S. 'Inclusion and choice: mutually exclusive principles in special educational needs?', in *Inclusive Education: Policy, Contexts and Comparative Perspectives*, F. Armstrong, D. Armstrong and L. Barton (eds), London, David Fulton Publishers, 2000.

Tod, J. 'IEPs: inclusive educational practices?', *Support for Learning* 14 (4), 1999, pp. 184–8.

Tod, J. and Blamires, M. *IEPs – Speech and Language*, London, David Fulton Publishers, 1998.

UNESCO *The Salamanca Statement and Framework for Action on Special Needs Education*, New York, UNESCO, 1994.

Wedell, K. 'Points from the SENCo-Forum: putting inclusion into practice', *British Journal of Special Education* 27 (2), 2000, p. 100.

Zigmoid, N. and Baker, J.M. 'Full inclusion for students with learning disabilities: too much of a good thing?', *Theory into Practice* 35 (1), 1996, pp. 26–34.

Tim O'Brien

3.1 Introduction

Inclusion is a problematic concept, raising many questions, which as yet seem largely unanswered. Is inclusion intended to be a process that empowers all learners to take up their human and civil rights to participate within a unified learning community? If so, at what pace should it occur, what are the practical issues involved in making it happen and what demands does it place upon learners, teachers and the curriculum? Is it a process aimed at increasing democracy and establishing new cultural goals? If so, does this mean that special schools should be closed down because they further oppress those who, by definition, are already oppressed? Is it feasible to assume that our systems will become flexible enough to provide inclusion for all when clearly they cannot provide it for some?

The concept of full inclusion suddenly seems less of a possibility when it is confronted by the hard cases. By 'hard cases', I mean the people and systems that continually test the limits of the philosophy and practice of inclusion. As a result of the contra-indicating variables that they present, inclusion is instantly problematised. Hard cases emerge in any process of reform, they highlight the tensions that change creates. There are inherent dangers in adopting a stance whereby someone who questions the conceptual framework of inclusion is instantly construed as being opposed to children's rights. There are dangers too in keeping under wraps what might appear to be bad news in relation to inclusion for all. These attitudes allow hard cases to become the submerged reality of inclusion because they challenge its fundamental aims and potential to succeed. Moreover, it adds to the ontological fragility of inclusion and fails to recognise that we can learn from the hard cases. In this chapter I shall consider three types of hard cases:

1 hard case learners – testing the limits of inclusion at an individual learner level;
2 hard case teachers – testing the limits of inclusion at a classroom management level;
3 hard case systems – testing the limits of inclusion at an organisational level.

3.2 Polarisation and problematic concepts

The task of moving from integration to inclusion is seen as modernist and rights-based. It has its roots in the premise that all learners are educable and have a right to be educated. Where and how this education should take place is the current debate. However, it is not a new debate. In the United Kingdom, early child welfare pioneers were in favour of non-categorised schools as far back as the start of the 1900s (Thomas *et al.*, 1998). It is important to stress that inclusion should not be seen as a form of new-age integration – inclusion and integration are conceptually distinct: there are quantitative differences between them. Integration describes models where learners from different communities come together; the concept of inclusion proposes that learners should be active participators within one profoundly diverse community. Questions that attempt to define the meaning of inclusion, and consequently the aims of mainstream and special education, can promote a polarity of thinking where positional, or oppositional, posturing can take preference over interactive discourse. At one extreme in this process of staking out ground, we find those who seem to preach the litany of inclusion, unswerving in their aim to ensure that all learners in special education take up their right to learn alongside their mainstream peers. With almost religious fervour they aim to increase the headcount of inclusive placement. Thus, fast-track social justice can be attained. At the other extreme are those that appear to want to hijack yet another idealistic education bandwagon. The trouble with a bandwagon is that it can all too easily become a runaway train. Therefore, they propose a freeze on inclusion in order to develop a system that inevitably becomes more segregated. This is typified by market force principles where the myth of choice is offered within elitist structures.

Caught in the middle of this battle are some of the most vulnerable learners within the education system, their teachers, families and parents or advocates. The learners, particularly when they carry the special educational needs (SEN) label, can become casualties of the application of systemic abuse as decisions are made about their inclusion – or formal exclusion – by those who wield power over them. Their voice is rarely heard in the decision-making process that surrounds them (Garner, 1999) and it cannot be assumed that placement in a mainstream school will result in higher quality learning for them (Hornby, 1999). 'School' is a problematic concept too. Schools cannot operate within a vacuum in which all learning and decision-making is value-free and unaffected by cultural frameworks.

In recent years we have seen a developing international commitment towards creating inclusive schools. We must accept that this does not automatically mean that we are also creating inclusive classrooms. There is a substantial difference between *being there* and *learning there* (O'Brien, 2000). Inclusion depends on the latter. Schools may describe themselves as inclusive because they have created adaptable and suitably resourced environments. However, this is an example of inclusion taking place at an organisational level – the school is 'organisationally inclusive'. It does not necessarily mean that the school is also 'learning inclusive' – that inclusive teaching and learning are taking place within the classrooms. While the planning of inclusion must consider responses such as funding, class size, resources and other important factors, we must not be deflected from the critical issue: that children and young people attend school, be it special, mainstream, or a combination of both, so that they can learn. Learning must become the central focus of the inclusion agenda. Of course, there are smooth transitory experiences that demonstrate how successful inclusion can be. There are also hard case situations that provide a high level of tension. This tension is helpful. It enables us to conceptualise inclusion in an attempt to define what it is, is not, and might become – to develop principles, explore models and to establish its meaning. I accept that any process of defining requires thinking that is by nature exclusionary. However, meaning is interconnected and one powerful method of generating meaning is through contrast. I would assert that we can find out more about who is being included, and the concept of inclusion itself, by gazing analytically at who is being excluded.

3.3   Hard case learners

I am not using the term 'hard case' to criticise certain learners. I am searching for more clarity in relation to what choices are available and to whom, whether the inclusion process is intended to be all-encompassing, and whose needs in relation to quality of life and learning are really being considered. Hard case learners challenge the notion of inclusion for all by demanding that their unique learning difficulties are understood and their short- and long-term learning needs are met. Some of these learners are likely to be reminded that, for them, inclusion hinges upon the learning rights of other members of their learning community being safeguarded.

For some learners, especially those who feel the stigma of being labelled 'special' (Norwich, 1997), inclusion may be a desirable goal. Learners in special schools may feel embarrassment or shame about their schooling based upon how they perceive it in relation to mainstream provision. For example, learners who experience emotional and behavioural difficulties (EBD) might believe that attending a special school is their punishment for mainstream misdemeanours. They may harbour anxieties about attending mainstream school and, due to the depressing catalogue of their learning history, may have lost faith in a system that has previously rejected them (O'Brien, 1998). Their anxieties could relate to how the mainstream system can offer a new start and afford them respect. Such hard cases threaten aspects of inclusive ideology because they urge the school to justify inclusive practice by providing an answer to the question about what exactly the school is offering them that is better than they could receive elsewhere. Their own construct of themselves as learners, and as people, may cause them to fight against the inclusive process at the initial stages even though they may want desperately to succeed within it. If the systemic response is one that directs them to the nearest available exit door, then the process of full inclusion is evidently an illusion. For these hard case learners, often singled out and under senior management surveillance, the process of inclusion can so easily become one of 'in one end and out the other'. Some hard case learners will disappear from the school system completely and receive a minimal amount of tuition per week. The damaging reality for others is that there is no formal education available to them at all once they have been formally excluded. Some pre-empt this outcome and are represented among the statistics for national truancy and, in some situations, criminal offences too (DfEE, 1998a). This is not inclusion – it is disorientation and dislocation. Any such process of outgrouping will have a detrimental effect upon the development of inclusive communities.

3.3.1 A real-world scenario

Any individual whose learning styles and strategies require the consideration of certain pedagogical approaches and tools can be transformed into a hard case learner. This type of hard case emphasises that learner difference requires teaching difference. A real-world example of this involved a girl with Down's Syndrome who was receiving an inclusive placement at her local primary school. This example highlights many issues involved in enabling inclusion for individuals with complex needs. When the staff met her, she was very excited about attending their school. However, once in a mainstream context the initial positive picture became tainted. She started to become a hard case learner in that she began to challenge the inclusion that was deemed to be her human right –

a right that her parents had assertively argued for her to take up. Within weeks she was causing concerns for other learners, the teacher, and the learning support assistant (LSA). It would be reasonable to assume that she was also causing concerns for herself in that her own capacity to learn was being restricted. It was reported that she did not seem to understand instructions, was not making noticeable progress in reading, was losing self-confidence and was removing herself, apparently at random, from the classroom. Her relationships with her peers ranged from didactic to fractious. Those who were managing her learning were feeling de-skilled. They would have been helped by the knowledge that learners like her, for developmental reasons, might typically benefit from a pedagogical approach which involves a high level of visual sequencing and an errorless starting point (Wishart, 1996). In this case there was an urgent requirement for staff support and training in areas relating to models of learning and in understanding communication needs. The cost analysis was also high in terms of the increasing lack of professional confidence. It is likely that, due to her perceived intractable difficulties, this particular girl will return to special school at the point when she is old enough to attend mainstream secondary school. She will have been offered a taste of inclusion but will never be given the full menu.

There are many other hard case learners. Those who deal with the rights/choice dilemma by not consenting to take part in inclusion in a mainstream school are an example. However, it is possible for any learner who has spent time in special schooling to become hard case in an inclusive setting. This is because inclusion presents a learner with a reflexive statement of identity and involves factors that are beyond cognition. Complex emotional and social factors come into play when your sense of belonging has been created in a segregated setting and you have to create a new identity within an inclusive culture.

3.4   Hard case teachers

The teacher has immense power over setting the limits of inclusion within their own classroom and school. Learners and parents contribute to the establishment of these limits too. This is why the inclusion process, and the debate surrounding it, must become more inside out and less outside in. By 'inside out' I mean that it should be driven by, and responsive to the voices of learners, teachers and parents. By 'outside in' I refer to it being driven by, and responsive to, the voices of policy-makers and legislators. Currently, there appears to be an imbalance in favour of the latter. Some would propose that a partnership between the two would be the ideal arrangement. The problem here is that 'partnership' itself is developing hard case connotations. It is in danger of becoming another myth – especially when relationships are presented as equitable even though they are clearly reinforced by the structural and personal dynamics of power and powerlessness that are generated by institutions or embedded within them.

Many teachers think in a manner that is flexible and fluid, enabling inclusive learning to take place. Some seem to intuitively understand what a learning task looks like from the perspective of a learner – a vital professional skill for enabling inclusion. Unfortunately, some teachers think in fixed ways. This may be due to a lack of response to meeting their professional training needs but, whatever the reason, rigid thinking makes them hard cases. They may construct a concept of their professional self that remains absolute no matter what occurs in the world around them. This might be viewed as an indicator of a need for a change of school, or even profession, but it could also be seen as an entirely understandable response to the overwhelming demands and changes that have been imposed upon teachers over recent decades – often without consultation. Some teachers identify categorisations of learners whom they are willing or unwilling to teach. This makes them hard cases too. Guiney (2000) proposes that some teachers carry implicit models of individual needs that they 'do' and do not 'do'. A teacher may 'do' learners with physical disabilities as their contribution towards inclusion, but will not 'do' learners who present challenging behaviour and make their professional life far more stressful than they would like it to be. Such attitudes, as well as preventing the development of inclusive classrooms, can promote negative and stereotypical assumptions about disability and learning difficulty. Practitioners will recognise that there are hard case teachers who exercise institutionalised power by becoming active catalysts for the formal exclusion of certain types of learners.

The inside of a teacher's head is the key resource for inclusion because the starting point for inclusive learning begins when a teacher reflects upon how they create educational reality – how they make meaning out of their world. How they define, for example, inclusion, pedagogy, curriculum, knowledge, truth and autonomy will certainly have a direct influence upon their practice. Inclusive practice and inclusive thinking are interrelated. There has to be a reflection upon whether learner needs supersede teacher needs, and in what contexts. This is challenged, and can be undermined, by the teacher who may not see their role as being one of working within a framework that extends beyond their own well-being. Inclusion involves power sharing and a concern for equity and this can be precarious ground for a hard case teacher to stand upon. It also gives the teacher a wider responsibility beyond the daily timetable and subject syllabus.

3.4.1 Selective responsibility

It is possible to envisage a hard case teacher existing as a subject teacher in a secondary school where inclusion appears to be 'taking a grip'. The school already compartmentalises teacher roles by separating them into two main organisational systems: academic and pastoral. In this scenario the teacher identifies a long-standing attachment to the academic system. The response to the process of inclusion is as follows: 'I am a subject teacher, I chose to become a teacher so that I can teach my subject. I do not want to encounter pupils with behaviour problems; they are not my responsibility. The pastoral system should deal with them. I do not want to encounter pupils with learning difficulties; they are not my responsibility either. The learning support teachers or "inclusion co-ordinator" should deal with them. I did not become a teacher so that I could teach pupils with special needs...' and so it goes on. This type of view exists in schools. There may well be an argument for the development of a model where teachers with such an attitude do not work in inclusive classrooms. This would enable those who wish to teach learners with diverse learning needs to do so. However, inclusion instantly transforms itself into exclusion when teachers overtly select whose learning they are, and are not, responsible for among the learners who are *already* in their classroom. We may come to discover that the design and application of some models of performance-related pay – and their potential for hierarchical manipulation in future years – will ultimately work against inclusion and add to this difficulty.

Teachers can become hard cases when they support the view that learning difficulties are fundamentally within-child factors that remain the same despite the context and setting in which the learner learns. Identifying difficulties as deficits that are located within the person becomes a particular issue in enabling inclusion for learners who experience EBD. Croll and Moses (2000) note the 'widespread' view of professionals that those learners who present challenging behaviour should be educated in separate provision. They emphasise that inclusion is seen as most problematic when teachers teach pupils who are described as 'disturbed'.

This loosely applied label, as with other forms of labelling, directs our thinking towards the interactive or internal causation and construction of difficulty, where responsibility for the difficulty lies and what provision might reduce or intensify the difficulty. The use of 'disturbed' as a descriptor implies a psychiatric problem that is difficult to alter through educational intervention. Hence so-called 'wonder drugs' can become validated and uncontested as the first port of call for controlling behaviour within educational settings. The tensions between teaching and treatment are exposed in such situations (O'Brien, 1996). There is also an implication that it is rational to assume that people who are disturbed will present with behaviour that is disturbing. As a consequence, accepting professional responsibilities for altering a difficulty might be reduced, producing the potential for the development of a culture where learners are blamed for, or even demonised because of, the difficulties that they experience. Once again, vulnerable learners are the losers.

Some teachers, due to frustration and exhaustion, may well sign up to the category 'I am committed to inclusion *but* ...' They indicate the need for support and training. This could help to remove them from the emotional wasteland where they feel that they have exhausted every strategy and yet they still encounter learners whose needs they feel they cannot meet and the like of whom they have never seen before. To prevent the emergence of intentional or unintentional hard case teachers, we must address the large-scale and wanton abandonment of special needs training that has occurred over recent years. One solution would involve offering substantive input on special needs education and inclusion issues in initial teacher education. Another could be the provision of optional courses for qualified teachers who wish to develop the skills, knowledge and understanding required for working successfully in inclusive classrooms. To be supportive of change you need to be supported through change.

3.5 Hard case systems

The systems I refer to are those channels through which a learner's rights can be offered and choices can be made. The rights of learners can be viewed in many ways, for example, depending upon how we define what constitutes a 'disability' (DfEE, 1999). Over recent years we have seen a move towards a less segregated and more inclusive education system. Although inclusive systems aim to maximise opportunities for all, we cannot assume that they are value neutral. Many systems are founded upon, and continue to promote, 'normal' patterns of physical, emotional and cognitive development. Nor can we assume that organisational features do not impact upon a teacher's ability to make decisions and execute routines in the classroom. An analysis of the link between organisation (systems) and operationalisation (teaching) can illuminate how schools themselves can be the source of teaching difficulties as well as learning difficulties. Inclusive systems do not set arbitrary parameters upon who is entitled to learn within them and do not label some people as being of less human worth than others. This paradigm shift, from exclusive to inclusive, places great demands upon the collective consciousness of those who are responsible for learning. It challenges them to reflect upon who should and does receive inclusive provision, what criteria are used to enable that provision to be put in place and what the ultimate goal of the provision should be.

3.5.1 Include me out

Why is it that some systems become hard case and lose their flexibility? Exploring the contradictions between government ideologies and their application may provide some answers. The Green Paper asserts the right of the pupil with SEN to be educated in a mainstream school wherever possible while also emphasising that inclusion is *'a process not a fixed state'*. One favourable point for hard case systems, even though it is worryingly vague, is that there appear to be no clear boundaries for this process. Thus hard case systems can define hard case learners in order to keep them out. The Green Paper also asserts a parent's right to 'express a preference for a special school' if they believe it can meet their child's needs. Preference, not choice, is on offer here. Expressing a preference involves a 'win or lose' outcome. You may, or may not, get what you want, it is not a choice – that is the deal.

DfEE, 1997, p. 44, para. 3

The 1993 Education Act (para. 160) also supports parents in expressing a preference for their child to be educated in a school 'which is not a special school'. For your child's education to take place in a mainstream school, certain conditions need to be satisfied. The child must have access to relevant provision and resources but – and this is the key point for hard case systems – the placement should not impinge upon the provision of 'efficient' education for the children with whom she or he is being educated. This represents the case for the prosecution when hard case systems assert their right to self-preservation by preventing entry to, or formally excluding, hard case learners. For hard case learners already in the school the concept of 'sin bins' has recently re-emerged. Pupils 'with EBD' are removed from their peers to receive education in separate within school support units. In reality, so called 'sin bins' can become used as contamination containers, thus implying that there is a viral effect associated with learners who experience EBD. This is a hard case response to a hard case problem. The absence of fluidity of thought results in these learners being included out instead of being included in.

3.5.2 Learning links

The Green Paper also outlines a new role for special schools. A main feature of this role involves mutual co-operation with mainstream schools. Teachers in special schools are seen to be in an ideal position to support mainstream teachers through the inclusion process. There is an inherent assumption here that by virtue of teaching in a special school you are doing something different or additional to your mainstream colleagues. It is also assumed that you are able to offer training in whatever it is that is 'special' about teaching in a special school. Such an assumption cries out for empirical evidence as to whether a special needs pedagogy does exist (Lewis and Norwich, 2000). If it does, it is vital to establish whether it is context transferable. The proposal of increased links is taken up more actively in the 'Programme of Action' (DfEE, 1998b). Special schools are

DfEE, 1998b, p. 25, para. 11

encouraged to be *outward looking centres of excellence* as they become an integral part of the inclusive system. The intention is to require Local Education Authorities to provide details, within school organisation plans, of proposed developments in this area. Special schools are given a remit through which it is possible to evolve new methodologies enabling them to become a complementary, as well as a compensatory, resource for mainstream schools. This represents such a positive opportunity for special schools to take a creative role in the development of inclusive systems. It may also help combat the external perception that teachers only work in special education because they are icons of martyrdom. A change of focus from a search for their patience and kindness in saintly proportions to an analysis of what their common or specialised pedagogy might be would be most welcome. The opportunity to develop systems for cross-site and cross-curriculum practice has to be grasped. It could enable support, information, experience, models, understandings, strategies, solutions and skills to be shared. Without the development of such learning links there will be a further isolation of special schools and a reinforcement of the notion that learners with 'special' needs require curriculum 'support' – usually offered via a fragmented curriculum – whereas other learners require curriculum 'enrichment'.

3.5.3 Reconstruction in the market place

In the name of improving standards in schools we have seen the onset of a neurosis about assessing attainment rather than acknowledging achievement. This has been driven by market-force principles with their increasing focus upon outcomes that promote individualism over individuality. One example in the UK is the publication of league tables of national examination and test results. This has created the context for the following scenario to be possible. A primary school is inspected and complimented upon its ability to be responsive to a diverse range of learning needs. It is reported to be an indicator of the high quality of teaching within the school. This is publicised within the local community and the school is perceived as being excellent. A few months after the inspection, the test results are published and the school appears almost at the bottom of the LEA league table. External perceptions of the quality of teaching alter instantly. Recently excellent, it is now believed to be unsatisfactory. This school, in being so welcoming of pupils with SEN and so good at meeting diverse needs, has suffered the consequences of a low reputation within its wider community. The tensions between ideology and reality are self-evident. To deal with this dilemma the school is forced away from a philosophy that responds to *'the productive interplay'* of individual and group difference. Indeed, it becomes intimidated by it and undervalued because of it. Suffocated by an exclusive and competitive model of raising standards and victims of a dog-eat-dog survival culture between local schools, inclusive philosophy and practice are abandoned. Unwilling to suffer the professional degradation of being seen as a school where incompetent teachers provide an unacceptable quality of learning, it refuses to take such a high ratio of learners with 'special needs' in future. Having once been seen as valued members of a diverse community, these learners are reconstructed. They are now seen as being unlikely to achieve the top grades in tests, with the added potential to disrupt the learning of others, requiring the dumbing-down of the curriculum and demanding unreasonable amounts and levels of individual planning. Amidst the competitive culture and social goals of the market place who will accept such learners? For them, the zone of zero tolerance awaits.

Daniels, 1998

The rhetoric of full inclusion does not sit comfortably next to the reality of hard case systems that create the conditions for the growth of an inclusion underclass. This underclass already exists and is composed of those learners whom the mainstream system can or will not accommodate. Research data suggest that this headcount is likely disproportionately to contain African-Caribbean adolescent males (Majors *et al.*, 1998), those labelled as having SEN and those who experience potential instability in their lives as a result of situations such as living in care.

3.6   Inclusion: more than headcount

The key component of an inclusive school is not the total sum of those who are included in it – the inclusive headcount – but its ability to provide inclusive learning. The Salamanca Statement itself (UNESCO, 1994) clearly indicates that 'regular schools with an inclusive orientation' will have certain factors that help them to succeed. This *orientation* and what it does or does not look like is fundamental to the development of models of inclusion. One element of the orientation is a focus upon a 'child-centred' pedagogical approach. To provide this approach the learning environment must respond to individuals, both as unique people and as members of groups. It must also recognise how they learn. The system should continually prompt questions about who learns best, in what way, in what settings and why this should be so?

As the critical mass of the inclusive curriculum expands, the critical differences between learners increases. 'Curriculum' is yet another problematic concept. The curriculum is a values vehicle, and how it is conceived and perceived is an important dimension in providing inclusive learning. Inclusive practice can become goal-blocked if the curriculum is seen to be solely the subject components of the timetable. This only reinforces the inflexibility that characterises hard cases. The curriculum comprises all intended and unintended learning experiences that take place in and through the school. It enables all learners to manipulate knowledge as, in the process of learning, they reconstruct its topography. For the curriculum, expectations are high. It is expected to be able to counteract urban and rural social and economic deprivation. It is also expected to develop a learner's sense of belonging by contributing to how individuals construct a notion of self.

I have proposed that inclusive schools must offer more than inclusive placement (being there) and focus upon the provision of inclusive learning (learning there). This is because inclusive learning recognises and connects with the individuality of learners. It is interactive and mediated for you, and on your behalf, by peers – including peers with additional educational needs – your parents and teachers. Inclusive learning offers contexts where all learners can become teachers and all teachers can become learners. It is grounded learning (O'Brien and Guiney, 2001). It is grounded in who you are, your sense of worth, how you learn and the pace at which you learn. Inclusive learning moves beyond cognition: considering social, emotional and pedagogical factors that influence learning.

We have to answer, with integrity, the questions about where and how a learner learns best. Is it realistic, or morally right, to expect all learners to be able to learn in mainstream schools when they may receive a higher quality education through, for example, dual registration with a special school that provides interdependent links with a mainstream counterpart? Hard cases suggest that degrees of deconstruction within the current education system are necessary for inclusion to succeed. A less assimilationist and more pluralistic approach could provide situations where larger sites offer negotiated and combined learning programmes that take place in whatever grouping is in the best interest of learners. In such a model, learners with profound and multiple learning difficulties, for example, could be offered various modes of dignified engagement while not denying their complex learning and health needs. This could also have positive benefits in the emotional growth of the learners (Shevlin and O'Moore, 2000) and as a consequence the system will also flourish.

3.7   Conclusion

Inclusion, like teaching and learning, is inherently risky. We can increase our ability to enable inclusion, and promote a philosophy that moves beyond the tolerance of difference into an acceptance of diversity, by learning from the hard cases. There is a need for a more comprehensive, interactive and critical discourse about inclusion and hard cases force this to occur. They remind us that inclusion is a long-term process and not a short-term event. They raise questions about the meaning of inclusion and who benefits most from inclusive practice. When schools, in great numbers, begin to claim that they are inclusive, this is not an indicator that we have succeeded in creating inclusive systems. Verifiable evidence, gathered through data collection, can begin to show if classrooms are inclusive too. This will enable us to explore and, if necessary, challenge assumptions about the nature of inclusion for groups and individuals. It will also validate how schools support teachers and learners in understanding the learning process. Without a focus upon learning we will continue with the depressing proliferation of national and local systems that are far more explosive than they will ever be inclusive.

References

Croll, P. and Moses, D. 'Ideologies and utopias: educational professionals' view of inclusion', *European Journal of Special Needs Education*, 15, (1), 2000, pp. 1–12.

Daniels, H. 'Researching issues of gender in special needs education', in *Articulating with Difficulty: Research Voices in Inclusive Education*, P. Clough and L. Barton (eds), London, Paul Chapman, 1998.

Department for Education and Employment *Excellence for All Children: Meeting Special Educational Needs*, London, The Stationery Office, 1997.

Department for Education and Employment *Truancy and School Exclusion: Report by the Social Exclusion Unit*, London, The Stationery Office, 1998a.

Department for Education and Employment *Meeting Special Educational Needs: A Programme of Action*, Sudbury, DfEE,1998b.

Department for Education and Employment *From Exclusion to Inclusion: A Report of the Disability Rights Task Force on Civil Rights for Disabled People*, London, DfEE, 1999.

Garner, P. *Pupils with Problems: Rational Fears ... Radical Solutions?*, Stoke on Trent, Trentham Books, 1999.

Guiney, D. 'The individual education plan' in *Special Needs and the Beginning Teacher*, P. Benton and T. O'Brien (eds), London, Continuum, 2000.

Hornby, G. 'Inclusion or delusion: can one size fit all?', *Support for Learning* 14 (4), 1999, pp. 152–7.

Lewis, A. and Norwich, B. *Mapping a Pedagogy for Special Educational Needs*, Monograph, University of Exeter and University of Warwick, 2000.

Majors, R., Gillborn, D. and Sewell, T. 'The exclusion of black children: implications for a racialised perspective', *Multicultural Teaching* 16 (3), 1998, pp. 35–7.

Norwich, B. 'Exploring the perspectives of adolescents with moderate learning difficulties on their special schooling and themselves: stigma and self-perceptions', *European Journal of Special Needs Education* 12 (1), 1997, pp. 38–53.

O'Brien, T. 'Challenging behaviour: challenging an intervention, *Support for Learning* 11 (4), 1996, pp. 161–4.

O'Brien, T. *Promoting Positive Behaviour*, London, David Fulton Publishers, 1998.

O'Brien, T. 'Increasing inclusion: did anyone mention learning?', *REACH, The Journal of Special Needs Education in Ireland*, 14 (1), 2000, pp. 2–11.

O'Brien, T. and Guiney, D. *Differentiation in Teaching and Learning: Principles and Practice,* London, Continuum, 2001.

Shevlin, M. and O'Moore, M. 'Creating opportunities for contact between mainstream pupils and their counterparts with learning difficulties', *British Journal of Special Education*, 27 (1), 2000, pp. 29–34.

Thomas, G., Walker, D. and Webb, J. *The Making of the Inclusive School,* London, Routledge, 1998.

United Nations Educational, Scientific and Cultural Organisation (UNESCO) *The Salamanca Statement and Framework for Action on Special Needs Education* (adopted by the World Conference on Special Needs Education: Access and Quality, Salamanca, Spain), New York, UNESCO, 1994.

Wishart, J. 'Avoidant learning styles and cognitive development in young children with Down's Syndrome', in *New Approaches to Down's Syndrome*, B. Stratford and P. Gunn (eds), London, Cassell, 1996.

Philip Garner

4.1 Introduction

For a number of years I have held a view that special educational needs
(SEN) training and professional development have not kept pace with
either the new thinking on, or the underpinning statutory guidance for,
educational inclusion. Both aspects of teacher development are awash with
hyperbole and paradox in equal measure. For example, the publication of
Meeting Special Educational Needs: A Programme of Action (DfEE, 1998)
highlighted new opportunities for professional development and training in
the field of SEN. It talks in explicit terms of the importance of developing
an appropriately skilled set of class teachers, special needs co-ordinators
(SENCos) and learning support assistants (LSAs) to meet the various
educational needs of children who are educated in either mainstream or
segregated (special school) settings.

However, the Programme of Action is being operationalised in a most
unpromising context. There has been no formal undergraduate teaching
award with an SEN specialism for almost ten years in England and Wales.
There is also an almost total absence of fully funded places for teachers on
full-time award-bearing courses during their careers. In consequence, much
professional development has been reduced to *'one-off days of quick-fix staff
training which ... frequently employs visiting experts, who may, but often do
not, have experience and expertise in special educational needs'*.

McLaughlin and
Tilstone, 2000, p. 60.

These events offer little opportunity for critical reflection concerning
personal beliefs and decision-making in SEN. The same can be said of the
existing pattern of award-bearing courses in SEN. Teachers and others
usually follow these on a part-time basis: the pressures of day-to-day work
in the classroom frequently mean that too little time is available for them
to critically examine their own work. Moreover, these courses now fall
under the concentrated gaze of the Teacher Training Agency, who require
demonstrations of 'impact' as a measure of a course's viability. In such
circumstances one is inclined to ask whether enough is being done to
sustain practising teachers during this time of significant change.

The situation becomes even more depressing when turning to initial
teacher education (or initial teacher training (ITT) as I will refer to it
henceforth – for apposite reasons). Accordingly, the central premise of this

chapter is that the concept of inclusion, itself a deeply problematic notion, as other contributors in this book are suggesting, is unworkable at a practical level because of a persistent shortfall in requisite skills, experiences and values of teachers in mainstream schools. This is a direct result of the inadequate coverage of SEN and educational inclusion as themes within ITT courses. In consequence, an argument is made that inclusion will require a substantial reorientation in our thinking in respect of ITT. Underlying this is my belief that to promote inclusion in an era of competition – at every level of the education service – is an unforgivable deceit, in that it uses both disadvantaged learners, and their teachers, as pawns in a Machiavellian drive to secure power through moral authority. Thus, I will examine recent developments in ITT course provision in order to adumbrate the key shortfalls in student experience; these, I maintain, are core inhibitors to educational inclusion. Their continued neglect reflects badly upon policy-makers, providers and teachers alike. Most crucially, it impacts on the educational opportunities and life chances of those who have disabilities and learning difficulties.

4.2 The sad case of educational studies

Since 1988 considerable adjustment has had to be made to the nature of ITT course content to accommodate the demands for more substantial coverage of National Curriculum (NC) subjects. As a result, there has been a reduction in the amount of time available for reflection, based upon a critical and humanistic tradition. These have been summarised by Jordan and Powell as constituting a move:

> *'away from the conceptual understandings of the educational process that were provided by the four underpinning disciplines (psychology, history, philosophy and sociology) towards a skills-based model based on an analysis of teacher competencies'.*

1995, p. 120

Later these 'disciplines' were subsumed within a generic course, followed by full cohorts of student teachers on a compulsory basis: educational studies. Typically such courses would cover elements of the 'hidden' curriculum of schooling: equality, learning differences, pastoral care, values, citizenship, gender, race, class and culture among them. It was in this 'secret garden' that trainee teachers would normally be exposed to the values debate concerning individual differences and equity. Though by no means perfect, this was an arena in which reflection held sway, and the capacity to forge a personal vision for a life's work in education was promoted.

But in the new (post-1988) reality the principle of technical rationalism emerged, in which competencies in subject knowledge were emphasised and seen as the panacea for perceived shortcomings and a means of meeting the needs of capitalism at the expense of individual democracy (Hartley, 1991). A technical-rationalist approach views an understanding of the needs of the child as secondary to an understanding of a body of subject-knowledge to be 'delivered': the 'secret garden' became the 'public allotment'. The Department for Education (DfE), officially confirmed the status of this approach by indicating that:

> 'the focus of ITT should be on the subject knowledge and the practical skills required by newly qualified teachers, which equip them to teach effectively and [which] are the foundation for further professional development'.
>
> DfE, 1993, p. 5

In the face of the all-encompassing demand for competence in subject knowledge, which was by the same token something which could be easily (if arbitrarily) 'measured' by output, the person-centred reflection at the heart of educational studies stood little chance of prevailing. Gradual encroachment on the time available to cover educational studies themes was reduced; the inference, to a student population who were inexorably becoming Thatcher's Children, was that issues such as equal opportunities and special educational needs were seen as being of little consequence.

The impact of the NC on schools was mirrored in Institutes of Higher Education (IHEs). The importance of academic subject teaching was confirmed. Core NC subjects received significant allocations of time on ITT courses followed by other, non-core areas. As the licence-to-teach of IHEs came to be increasingly measured, by the TTA, by outputs largely built around subject skills and competencies, ITT course organisers and tutors had little option but to concur with central government requirements for standardisation of what was being taught. Deviation from this meant the wrath of OfSTED and the removal of recognition as a provider of ITT courses. Courage is a characteristic of the few in education: not surprisingly ITEs in the main succumbed or were engulfed in the trample for approval (and the student number allocation, which followed).

One illustration of the impact of the NC in teacher education can be seen in the failure of IHEs to cater for the training needs of teachers in relation to EBD pupils. Cooper et al., in summarising the post-Elton position concerning ITT and pupils whose behaviour caused concern, stated that:

'Teachers in general are unprepared by their initial training, and by in-service training arrangements for dealing with emotional and behavioural difficulties ... and specialist teachers in the field have been shown to place their requirement for further training in the area high on their list of priorities'.

1994, p. 3

In a very large part this refers to both the curriculum that is offered to such children and the way in which it is delivered. A particularly important element of this is that part of the school curriculum which provides 'pupils with problems' with the opportunity to examine aspects of their own personal development – an area of activity which is frequently referred as the 'pastoral curriculum'.

The consistent failure of ITT courses to provide much in the way of input regarding the 'pastoral curriculum' has serious implications. EBD pupils are a major focus of controversy in the inclusion debate. Recent surveys (Garner, 1998a, 1998b) suggest that this pupil grouping is far less likely to be considered for inclusion than any other is by mainstream teachers. Over fifty years ago the School Health regulations of 1945, in defining the term 'maladjusted pupil', stated that these were children who *require special educational treatment in order to effect their personal, social or education readjustment'.* Such 'readjustment', according to Laslett (1977) is unlikely to be achieved by *'teaching the same subjects as the ordinary school rather differently with different teachers'.* Laslett argued that it is success in the 'social curriculum' which underpins any academic progression within NC subjects. He maintains that: *'these other successes come about through achievements the children make in forming and sustaining successful relationships with others, and in changing unsatisfactory patterns of behaviour',* adding the telling remark that *'I am not certain at all that this learning can be encompassed within the [formal] curriculum'.*

1977, p. 111

Finally, in the post-1988 era of curriculum imposition, it may well be worth noting G.K. Galbraith's observation, quoted by Storm that *'Just as truth ultimately serves to create a consensus, so in the short run does acceptability. Ideas come to be organised around what the community as a whole or particular audiences find acceptable'.* We have to recognise that what occurs in IHEs does so with the approbation of society as a whole. The current preoccupation remains firmly rooted in 'excellence' as determined by curricular performances in core NC subjects, which are measured on output. Under such conditions ITT provision is doing nothing to promote inclusive thinking on the part of NQTs, as their performance is

1973, p. 113

unlikely to be assessed, at anything other than a superficial level, on the merits of their work with pupils with learning difficulties.

4.3　School-based training in SEN: the law of adhocracy

The shift towards school-based training marks a second area of concern for the advancement of an inclusive agenda among students following ITT courses. Prior to 1988 a student's school experience was obtained alongside considerable practice-related study within university and college departments of education, supported by a series of informally arranged school placements. Official thinking was that ITT courses had little relation to what really went on in schools – a view which was not unchallenged – Circulars 9/92 (DfE, 1992) and 14/93 (DfE, 1993) resulted in important 'changes' in these arrangements. Circular 14/93, for example, stated that: 'schools should play a much larger and more influential role in course design and delivery' and that the Secretary of State intends that the increased contribution of schools to teacher-training courses, offered by higher education institutions, should be reflected in the transfer of resources from the institutions to their partner schools.

DfEE, 1993, p. 12

The ongoing effect of such a move, towards what has effectively become an 'apprenticeship model' involving 'on-the-job training', has been increasingly felt both by students and by newly qualified teachers (NQTs) in terms of the SEN dimension. One obvious result is that even less time is available for consideration of important conceptual issues in SEN, including debates on the efficacy of inclusive approaches with SEN populations. Henceforth students would rely upon picking up messages from the prevailing culture and ethos of the school in which they were placed for 'school experience'. But it is widely acknowledged that the concept of inclusion – as, indeed, of special educational needs itself – is received with various degrees of understanding and commitment across the teaching profession; and, commensurately, it varies in emphasis from school to school. In cases where an enthusiastic SENCo and student-mentor are in post, a student on placement is likely to receive sound and structured inputs on the basics of SEN; in similar terms, the concept of inclusion is likely to be presented positively as one of entitlement and social justice. However, the move towards school-based training needs also to be seen in the context of recent surveys of SENCos. They have reported a massive increase in workload since the adoption of the Code of Practice (DfE, 1994), and, in consequence, a lack of availability to act as mentors to either students or to NQTs (Garner, 1996a; Lewis, 1995).

Consideration also needs to be given to the fact that, as OfSTED inspectors are given to noting apparent wide variations in the quality of teaching and learning in schools, students may commensurately face a lottery as to the quality of their SEN experience in schools. The Special Educational Needs Training Consortium (SENTC), commenting on this state of affairs in 1996, reported that *'Much therefore depends on the quality of SEN policy and practice in the partnership schools in which the student is placed. Yet HMI/OfSTED reports have in the past been critical of SEN practice in mainstream schools'.*

1996, p. 19

Many students, therefore, are likely to receive only nominal direct input on practical matters relating to such fundamental SEN issues as legislation, identification, assessment and behaviour management; they are much less likely to have opportunities to debate the principles and practicalities of inclusion.

Finally, recent surveys in the national press (*The Guardian*, 29 February 2000) indicate a forthcoming catastrophic problem in teacher supply. The current age-profile of teachers (primary and secondary) is worryingly high; with retirements and early retirements it is estimated that there will be a general shortfall of approaching 50 per cent by 2010. In a word, there will be a skills and capability haemorrhage in SEN; teachers who had the benefit of exposure to a more SEN-friendly teacher education experience will be lost to the profession. Their replacements, largely the product of subject-based, instrumentalist 'training', will simply provide the necessary respectable veneer to the perpetuation of a national disgrace; mere sticking plaster to a mortal wound.

4.4 Osmosis or ossification: permeation of SEN within ITE courses

The final theme delineating the negative landscape of teacher education and SEN is that of 'permeation'. This is a process by which SEN matters are subsumed within each element of an ITT course and become the responsibility of all tutors within an IHE-based teaching team. While this approach encourages all tutors to be involved more directly in SEN, there are huge difficulties of quality control. Mittler, for example, noted that, *'Permeation is by its very nature invisible and therefore difficult to monitor'* while an official view, even ten years ago, was that permeation has an *'insufficient foundation by way of specific course content'.*

Mittler, 1992

DES, 1990

The argument against a 'permeated' approach to SEN content-provision in ITT is overwhelming. ITT students have repeatedly complained that failure to obtain discrete, SEN-specific input is a major handicap to them once they qualify (Garner, 1996b). In much the same way that a school-based model of ITT results in variable (and varied) student experience, so too the permeated approach becomes the sort of lottery which Camelot would be proud of. Up and down the country, in one IHE after another, course leaders struggle to embed SEN within subject studies. Tutors with SEN backgrounds attempt to provide input more reminiscent than ever of a 'tips-for-teachers' approach; and, where courses function without SEN-specific staffing, coverage of important basic issues goes to the wall.

This state of affairs prevails at both undergraduate (BA/QTS and BEd) as well as post-graduate (PGCE) levels. The latter case is illustrative of the value-free, barren and ultimately destructive way in which many courses of ITT are currently structured. A typical scenario has an SEN tutor delivering (the term is highly apposite in this respect) a formal one-hour input on SEN – the single occasion when students would benefit from specialist-led involvement. At best this might comprise a series of anecdotes about learning difficulty that can be strung together, supported by some reading material and further references. The prospect of engaging in critical and lively reflection about the 'controversial issues' (Hornby *et al.*, 1997) is about as likely to happen as a reconsideration of the structure, format and outcomes of teacher education itself. Net result? NQTs with superficial knowledge, considerable prejudice and minds that are likely to remain firmly shut in the face of their struggle with the demands of an induction year.

4.5 Remedial education, slow learners, SEN or inclusion: action not labels

Together with a colleague, I have noted elsewhere (Davies and Garner, 1997) that:

> *'It appears that many of our European partners in particular have been more whole-hearted in their adoption of the Salamanca Statement (UNESCO, 1994) which argues that mainstream schools which adopt an "inclusive" approach for all children are the best placed to combat discrimination'.*

EASE, 1995

These sentiments have been echoed in the Declaration on Education for All (EASE, 1995), which affirmed that *'Teacher training should be more comprehensive and include the basic principles of the education of children with SEN in order to allow inclusive education.'* Closer adherence to these fundamental principles is marked in real terms by making resources (human, financial and temporal) available so that ITT courses are able, as a matter of course, to include a far more substantial element of both practical experience and theoretical input. In particular, they would assist in creating the necessary cultural conditions, in schools, for the consideration of inclusion as a viable approach to meeting the needs of all pupils.

Even at the present time, when the education service is benefiting from the involvement of teachers who have undertaken courses of ITT in an era when time was not one of the enemies of reflection, there is an urgent need to reformulate ITT provision for the sake of the future. In doing this two considerations will need to be at the forefront of our thinking: what is covered, in ITT courses, relating to SEN and inclusion; and how that coverage is organised, particularly that relating to school-based experience.

The emphasis on 'partnership' between schools and IHEs, currently being promoted, could provide a useful vehicle for development. For example, NQTs during their first years of teaching, should have some mechanism available to them to return to their ITT provider (or, by some form of national agreement, one local to their new place of work) in order to refine or extend specific SEN skills. These are often only apparent to students and their induction mentors in schools, once they begin teaching. The process could act as a 'learning guarantee' and could provide a useful way of assessing quality provision. Moreover, it could enhance effective working liaisons between SEN teachers in schools and SEN tutors in IHEs.

Urgent attention also needs to be paid to the failure of a 'permeated approach' of SEN in ITT courses. This can only be tackled if all tutors working in teacher education are made more aware of SEN issues, the underpinning legislative basis of provision for those who have learning difficulties, and of the kinds of interventions most likely to be effective with SEN children. There is, in particular, room for considerable updating via professional development in respect of inclusion and its impact. Moreover, there should be no teacher education provider without an experienced SEN tutor on its staff. This tutor could act both in terms of direct, SEN-related input but also as the fulcrum of SEN-specific staff development.

Nor should ITT courses fail to provide compulsory, long-term course components on matters relating to learning difficulties. This is not to advocate a separationist approach. On the contrary, such a strategy is needed to forestall the onset of subject-knowledge visigoths, rampant in teacher education since the Education Act, 1988. Such courses need to provide opportunities to consider key inclusion issues such as the psychology of learning, classroom pedagogy and an understanding of the socio-economic context of underachievement and disadvantage. Those involved in the debate might wish to be warned of the dangers that lie in wait, lest the Right hijacks a new set of proposals. Thus, Lawton and Chitty (1988) have referred to the bureaucratic versus the professional approach to curriculum building, suggesting that:

> 'Whereas the professional approach focuses on the quality of the input and the skills, knowledge and awareness of the teacher, the bureaucratic approach concentrates on output and testing. Whereas the professional approach is based on individual differences and the learning process, the bureaucratic approach is associated with norms or benchmarks, norm-related criteria and judgements based on the expectations of how a statistically normal child should perform. Whereas the professional curriculum is concerned with areas of learning and experience, the bureaucratic curriculum is preoccupied with traditional subject boundaries.'

1988, p. 202

The potential for using the skills and background of teachers working in special schools has long been acknowledged as important in ITT. Regrettably, special schools have almost wholly been excluded from partnership arrangements in ITT, with the result that the kinds of stereotypical responses to children educated in these contexts, reported, for example, by Garner (1994), are likely to prevail. IHEs need to grasp the nettle in this respect by promoting more widespread, formal collaboration with their local special schools. In doing this, it is essential that a more expansive version of 'inclusion' is adopted, in which special schools have a role, which is as much about advancing conceptual thinking as it is about providing hands-on expertise. Mainstream-special school partnership arrangements can thus be of mutual benefit for both establishments, while assisting in developing a more cohesive view of inclusion itself.

Providers of SEN within teacher education have, for some time, had 'the odds stacked against them' (Robertson, 1999). Now, with a dramatic focus being placed on inclusion in the widest sense, it seems that the time is right to commit to a vociferous campaign to secure a more equitable portion of time and resources for discrete SEN-inclusion provision in ITT courses. Some might argue that this is a paradox. I would counter this by reiterating the theme in this chapter: teacher education's coverage of SEN has, over the last ten years or so, represented a deceit. The deception has been, and continues to be, perpetrated on account of the 'fitness for purpose' of ITT courses which manifestly do not meet the real needs of NQTs and, ultimately, those of pupils with learning difficulties. Central government continues to peddle the lie that a 'qualified teacher' has at least covered the basic principles inherent to inclusion. Wrong: they continue to struggle with more rudimentary concepts such as SEN and integration. So what is still happening has the mark of a raging insult to children and young people with learning difficulty. They have been dispossessed through dogma: inclusion on the cheap is about the sum of it all. If, as those most closely involved in inclusion-related teacher education, we say goodbye to the benign, pupil-orientated notion of Mr Chips, it is all bound to end in tears. Above all else we should not be side-tracked down a blind alley of debating fatuous, pious and ultimately discriminating terminologies – however benign they might sound. What are needed, on the ground, are actions not words.

Acknowledgement

I would like to thank John Dwyfor Davies (University of the West of England, Bristol) for his insights and suggestions on some aspects of this chapter.

References

Cooper, P., Smith, C. and Upton, G. *Emotional and Behavioural Difficulties*, London, Routledge, 1994.

Croll, P. and Moses, D. *One in Five: The Assessment and Incidence of Special Educational Needs*, London, Routledge and Kegan Paul, 1985.

Davies, J. and Garner, P. (eds) *At the Crossroads: Teacher Education and Special Educational Needs*, London, David Fulton, 1997.

Department for Education *The Initial Training of Secondary School Teachers: New Criteria for Courses (Circular 9/92)*, London, DfE, 1992.

Department for Education *The Initial Training of Primary School Teachers: New Criteria for Courses (Circular 14/93)*, London, DfE, 1993.

Department for Education and Employment *Code of Practice on the Identification and Assessment of Special Educational Needs*, London, DfEE, 1994.

Department for Education and Employment *Meeting Special Educational Needs: A Programme of Action*, Sudbury, DfEE, 1998.

Department for Education and Science *Special Educational Needs: Report of the Committee of Enquiry into the Education of Handicapped Children and Young People*, London, HMSO, 1978.

Department for Education and Science *Discipline in Schools* (The Elton Report), London, DES, 1989.

Department for Education and Science *Special Educational Needs in Initial Teacher Training*, London, DES, 1990.

European Association of Special Education (EASE) *Declaration on Education for All*, Information from EASE, 2, Brussels, 1995.

Garner, P. 'Oh my God, help!: What newly qualifying teachers think of special schools', in *Whose Special Need?*, S. Sandow (ed.), London, Paul Chapman, 1994, pp.129–40.

Garner, P. 'A special education? The experience of newly qualified teachers during initial training', *British Educational Research Journal* 22 (2), 1996a, pp. 155–63.

Garner, P. 'Students' views on special educational needs courses in Initial Teacher Education', *British Journal of Special Education* 23 (4), 1996b, pp. 176–9.

Garner, P. *Developing a Professional Repertoire: Teachers' Views Regarding Desirable Attributes for Working with Children with Emotional and Behavioural Difficulties*, paper presented at the British Education Research Association symposium, Queen's University, Belfast, August, 1998a.

Garner, P. *'Dragging the Horse to Water: Secondary School Subject Teachers and Special Needs'*, European Conference on Educational Research, Llubljana, September, 1998b.

Gipps, C., Gross, H. and Goldstein, H. *Warnock's Eighteen Per Cent: Children with Special Needs in Primary Schools*, Lewes, Falmer Press, 1987.

Hartley, D. 'Democracy, capitalism and the reform of teacher education', *Journal of Education for Teaching* 17 (1), 1991, pp. 81–5.

Hornby, G., Atkinson, M. and Howard, J. *Controversial Issues in Special Education*, London, David Fulton, 1997.

Jordan, R. and Powell, S. 'Skills without understanding: a critique of a competency-based model of teacher education in relation to special needs', *British Journal of Special Education* 22 (3), 1995, pp. 120–4.

Laslett, R. *Educating Maladjusted Children*, London, Crosby, Lockwood and Staples, 1977.

Lawton, D. and Chitty, C. (eds) *The National Curriculum*, The Bedford Way Papers, London, London University, Institute of Education, 1988.

Lewis, A. *Special Needs Provision in Mainstream Primary Schools*, Stoke-on-Trent, Trentham, 1995.

McLaughlin, M. and Tilstone, C. 'Standards and curriculum: the core of curriculum reform', in *Special Education and School Reform in the United States and Britain*, M. McLaughlin and M. Rouse (eds), London, Routledge, 2000.

Mittler, P. 'Preparing all initial teacher training students to teach children with special educational needs: a case study from England', *European Journal of Special Needs Education* 7 (1), 1992, pp. 1–10.

Mittler, P. 'Special needs education in England and Wales', in *Teacher Education for Special Needs in Europe*, P. Mittler and P. Daunt (eds), London, Cassell, 1995.

Office for Standards in Education *The New Teacher in School*, London, HMSO, 1993.

Office for Standards in Education *Guidance on the Inspection of Primary Schools*, London, HMSO, 1996.

Robertson, C. 'Initial teacher education and inclusive schooling', *Support for Learning* 14 (4), 1999, pp. 169–73.

Special Educational Needs Training Consortium *Professional Development to Meet Special Educational Needs*, Stafford, SENTC, 1996.

Storm, M. 'The community and the curriculum', in *Deschooling*, I. Lister (ed.), Cambridge, Cambridge University Press, 1973.

UNESCO (1994) *The Salamanca Statement and Framework for Action on Special Needs Education*, Paris, UNESCO, 1994.

Chapter (5)

Entitlement or denial? The curriculum and its influences upon inclusion processes

Richard Rose and Marie Howley

5.1   Introduction

In recent years the debate concerning the future of education for pupils with special educational needs (SEN) has revolved around philosophical and socio-political arguments, with a focus upon the move to inclusion as a right for all pupils. The polemic which has characterised this discussion has resulted from a consideration of human rights, which has often compared the politics of disability with issues of race, class and gender (Mithaug, 1998). Similarly, opinions have been expressed that the inclusion debate has resulted from the need to recognise that special education has its origins in a desire on the part of policy-makers to exert control over a potentially disruptive section of the population which society has failed to understand (Oliver, 1988). Indeed, the history of treatment and attitudes towards people with a disability or special need within this country and further afield has been a far from honourable one (Rieser, 1990; Foucault, 1997).

This concentration upon the education of pupils with SEN as a rights issue has served a number of important functions. First, it has challenged assumptions with regards to the abilities of pupils with special needs to learn alongside, to interact with, and to share in the daily activities of their peers. The inclusion debate, by drawing attention to the need to provide for all pupils within the mainstream classroom, has caused teachers to examine their practices and to adopt approaches to address the needs of a wider range of pupils. The majority of pupils with SEN have always been found in mainstream classrooms. However, our understanding of the most effective means of providing an education for those who have the most challenging needs, the majority of whom are educated in special schools, remains far from complete.

Second, it has provoked discussion at all levels with regards to a future direction for special education. Philosophically there has been a fundamental shift away from the notion that special schools will be an automatic first choice of placement for pupils with significant special needs. Many Local Education Authorities (LEAs) have come to regard mainstream schools as the preferred option for all pupils. Terms such as 'ineducable' are no longer accepted, and there is a recognition that all children have an entitlement to an education that recognises and addresses their individuality. However, while major strides have been made in accepting the rights of all pupils, and in acknowledging their ability to learn, the majority of LEAs have retained, and in a few instances, increased their levels of special school provision.

The rationale for the retention of special schools needs careful consideration. If there has been a genuine shift towards an intention to provide mainstream education for all pupils, why has progress in achieving this been so slow? One suggestion is that there are some students who require a programme of learning which is different from, or over and above, that provided for the majority of pupils (Lieberman, 1992; Jenkinson, 1997). There are, for example, pupils with a sensory impairment who require to be taught via a communication media which can only be provided through specialist teachers or facilities. Similarly, some pupils, those described as having severe or profound and multiple learning difficulties, or at the extreme end of the autistic spectrum, may require teaching which provides a greater commitment to social skills and personal self-management than has been traditionally provided within mainstream schools. Farrell (1997) has suggested that for some of these pupils it is unlikely that *'full functional neighbourhood integration'* will become a reality. What is at question here is not the right of these pupils to receive an education, but rather the ability of the current education system to provide this within an appropriate framework built within the majority of mainstream schools. Indeed, for many mainstream schools their existing population of pupils with SEN already provides a challenge to current procedures and practices.

A focus upon the needs and rights of these pupils is to be welcomed, and writers who have promoted the inclusion debate have done a great service to the cause of both teachers and pupils. The literature on inclusion is both extensive and accessible, and provides a sound foundation for examining school structures and the conditions that may change the future education of all pupils. However, in order that progress in meeting the needs of all pupils may be achieved, there is a need for the inclusion debate to move forward into a new phase. The philosophical arguments have been well rehearsed, and must now give way to efforts to increase our understanding of what works in educating pupils with a wide range of special needs.

In an important review of the current state of special needs provision Dyson (1999) has described inclusion as being in a period of two discourses

(p. 48). The first of these he describes as a *discourse of ethics and rights*, concerned with gaining an understanding of pupil's rights and how these may best be addressed within the education system. The second he labels the *efficacy discourse*, which he describes as being concerned for the '*educational order of the inclusive school*', and an understanding of what works and why this might be the case. He recognises the current paucity of empirical research upon which sensible decisions can be made concerning the structure of mainstream schools in accepting a wider range of needs. He notes a general lack of ability to identify a pedagogical framework upon which to base a consistent practice that will benefit all pupils. Other writers (Feiler and Gibson, 1999; Hornby, 1999) have similarly identified the lack of empirical evidence to provide information with regards to the effectiveness of inclusion. We further contend that the argument in favour of an increase in research, should be extended to examine the effectiveness of all current approaches to educating pupils with SEN, regardless of the location in which such an education is provided.

If our concern is to ensure an improved education for all pupils, it is time to begin a more thorough and systematic investigation into teaching approaches which are most likely to attain this objective. In order to develop our understanding of effective teaching, and to promote those practices which will better enable all teachers to meet the challenges which confront them, we must avoid the establishment of narrowly focused pro- and anti-inclusionary camps. These become so entrenched in their own point of view that they lose all perspective and credibility. Söder (1997) suggests that research in the area of inclusion has been focused upon two aspects. The first he describes as evaluative, asking the question, is inclusion good or bad? The second is a normative approach, which addresses the issue of how inclusion can be made to work. While both of these approaches are important and have supplied researchers with critical points of discussion, Söder suggests that the time has come to move away from the evaluative debate, and to focus upon an examination of the most successful approaches to teaching pupils with special needs.

Paul and Ward (1996) have similarly argued that inclusion can be seen as a 'paradigmatic issue' into which opinion has divided into two distinct factions. The *comparison paradigm* considers comparisons made between pupils labelled as having SEN and those seen as their 'normal' peers. Within this context, judgements are made about the suitability of the individual pupil for placement in mainstream education based upon a vague criteria of 'normality'. The second model, traced back to Kant's categorical imperative, they describe as the *ethical paradigm*, which assumes that the acceptance of all individuals into a society that sees equality as its highest goal is morally immutable and cannot be subject to compromise. They believe that the inclusion debate is destined to remain at a philosophical level, and that inclusion will never be justified purely through scientific analysis of its application. However, they acknowledge that in order to advance our understanding of the pragmatics of inclusion, it will be necessary to develop a firmer research base upon which to make assertions regarding efficacy. In their plea for a greater analysis of pedagogy and its impact upon inclusion, they are acknowledging that we are some distance from being able to define what works best in the classroom. This being the case, we should exercise extreme caution when examining the current literature in the area of special education, and become far more critical of the basis upon which statements either for or against inclusion are made.

5.2   The shape of future needs provision

If we are to raise educational standards by addressing the needs of all pupils, we will need to draw upon the experience of all teachers. This must include those working in special schools and other forms of special provision who have committed themselves to working with those pupils who have traditionally been excluded from the mainstream. Many of these teachers have skills and understanding which have been critical in the development of teaching approaches and which have found favour with a significant number of parents who choose to send their children to a special school. To concentrate our attention solely upon the changes necessary in mainstream schools – while ignoring the significant advances in teaching pupils with special needs which have been made in special schools – is more likely to alienate policy-makers and advocates of full inclusion from those who have worked closely with the very pupils for whom inclusion is seen as providing the greatest benefit. In order to make progress in addressing this most complex of issues, it is necessary to draw upon all the experience and expertise available. This will include both teachers in mainstream and special schools. We should also be mindful of those teachers who through their work in specialist provision, often with pupils who have well-defined and specific needs such as autism or sensory impairments, have developed an understanding of how both integrated and segregated arrangements work. It may be that some of these colleagues can provide insights into the pragmatics of educating pupils in a variety of settings that other teachers do not have.

The Green Paper *Excellence for All Children* (DfEE, 1997) suggests that future provision for pupils with SEN will need to be developed along a continuum which includes the retention of some special schools. Such an assertion may be interpreted as recognition that there are some pupils for whom a mainstream placement may not be a realistic goal. However, in accepting that for the majority of pupils a mainstream education will be the model of future provision, there is a danger that if special schools do not change, they will become isolated, and for some pupils the opportunities for contact with their mainstream peers will be lost. Special schools will need to establish close links with the mainstream which have a clearly defined and mutually beneficial basis. While much of the enthusiasm for, and experience of, working with pupils who have the most complex needs has been retained within special schools, few mainstream schools have benefited from or had access to this expertise. In order to promote inclusion based upon learning processes, rather than upon location, there is a need to develop an education system which provides greater ease of transition between phases, and mutual support. This has been recognised in the Green Paper (DfEE, 1997) suggesting that teachers in special schools should provide specialist support for their colleagues in the mainstream. Such a proposal needs to be further developed, with the establishment of formal agreements, that build upon the *ad hoc* approach to co-operation which currently exists.

If future models of provision are based upon a continuum, there must be recognition that for some pupils transition from special to mainstream school, and vice versa, will become the norm. Schools will have a responsibility to ensure that such transitions can take place without adding further to the difficulties faced by the pupils concerned. Suggestions have been made (Jenkinson, 1997) that for some pupils a placement in two settings may be appropriate. This requires the establishment of cross-phase consistent procedures and also a requirement that schools examine their curriculum to ensure that all pupils have their individual needs recognised, providing content, teaching approaches, and resources to address these. Such a model will not be achieved without changes to the curriculum and its management. There must be a demand that the curriculum on offer in the special school, while complementing, and to a large extent overlapping that available in the mainstream, provides those 'specialist' elements which justify provision which is separate. If pupils are to be defined in terms of their curriculum needs, and these do not differ from those of their mainstream peers, there is no justification for education within a special school. Special schools must demonstrate that through a careful analysis of the needs of the individual they can tailor a curriculum which meets those needs which are unique to the individual, while recognising the rights of the pupil to be given access to mainstream peers.

This analysis extends beyond a simplistic assessment of pupil abilities. Logan and Malone (1998), in examining pupil reactions and participation in a range of instructional contexts, recognise that for many pupils with SEN alterations will need to be made to the traditional delivery modes encountered in mainstream classes. The practicalities of achieving such change will inevitably prove challenging to all schools and may be impossible for some. Adjusting the curriculum to meet the needs of all pupils will demand an increased flexibility in terms of placement arrangements. Special and mainstream schools working in tandem may be the only way of achieving such a supportive learning system.

5.3   The difficulties of working within existing curriculum models

It has been argued elsewhere (Rose, 1998a) that there are a significant number of pupils with SEN attending mainstream schools, who far from being included, find themselves isolated by teaching approaches and a curriculum that has failed to recognise their individuality. The curriculum in any school should exist as a means of supporting a framework through which learning can take place. In many schools this role has been reversed to a point where teachers are more concerned to address the requirements of a prescribed curriculum than planning to fully address the needs of pupils. Teachers feel under such pressure to ensure coverage of subject content, and to teach towards the accompanying assessments that they are in danger of overlooking the need to consider the range of teaching styles and approaches that will enable all pupils to learn at a pace suited to their needs. At its worst, the word curriculum has become synonymous with content, with little consideration given to the learning processes and pedagogical practices that can influence learning. Such practice has taken place, not through a reluctance or the inability of teachers to recognise and address individual needs, but through the development of a competitive educational climate which is concerned to measure effectiveness in terms of a narrow focus upon academic outcomes in a limited number of subjects. While the most effective teachers, and those with a commitment to SEN, will adapt and adjust their practice, a number will remain who will be less likely to respond positively to such a challenge.

Booth *et al.* (1997) have condemned what they perceive as reactionary policies which have driven the National Curriculum and the Office for Standards in Education (OfSTED) inspections. They suggest that increased competition between schools, based upon the drive to achieve good assessment results, is likely to lead to an increase in exclusion of pupils perceived as having an adverse effect upon successful outcomes. There is a danger that schools will place a high value upon those pupils who are able to achieve examination success, while being reluctant to recognise what may be perceived as the 'lesser' achievements of pupils who are working at levels below the expected 'norm'. Such a situation, far from promoting inclusion, is more likely to prove an obstacle to the development of good practice. It is equally likely to alienate teachers who have endeavoured to provide recognition for pupils with SEN through the development of alternative and more student-focused accreditation systems.

When the National Curriculum was introduced, it was heralded as a curriculum for all. Entitlement was proclaimed as the means by which all pupils would be recognised under the same curricular umbrella. Such an assertion was welcomed by teachers in special schools, many of whom developed approaches and materials which enabled pupils to gain access to subjects which had previously lain unexplored in many special schools (Carpenter *et al.*, 1996; Rose *et al.*, 1994). What was perceived as being a new dawn recognising the rights of all pupils to a broad, balanced and relevant curriculum has unfortunately been derailed through a failure to maintain the intentions which were espoused for the National Curriculum on its inception. The intention to provide a broad curriculum for pupils which includes the National Curriculum has in some instances been forgotten in the rush to ensure that a concentration on core subjects leads to acceptable assessment results for the majority.

Curriculum Guidance 3 (NCC, 1990) was seen by many as providing a sensible and balanced approach to the development of a curriculum which could meet the needs of all pupils. While asserting the importance of the National Curriculum which would be at the heart of all school curriculum models, this document recognised that for all pupils schools would need to provide much more. There was an acknowledgement that schools need to address subjects beyond the ten core and foundation subjects. Similarly, an emphasis upon cross-curricular elements, described as being 'concerned with the intentional promotion of pupils' personal and social development through the curriculum as a whole,' was seen by many teachers as the bedrock for developing a curriculum which recognised the specific needs of their pupils. Writing shortly after the introduction of the National Curriculum, Ashdown *et al.* (1991) in referring to pupils with severe learning difficulties stated that:

> *'Showing that those pupils with SLD can be given access to the National Curriculum will be a means of ensuring that more is done to maintain all pupils within the framework of the National Curriculum and avoid the use of the exception clause [by which pupils could be taken out of some or all aspects of the National Curriculum]. There will be modification but that is nothing new to special educators. We have always modified the work we present to pupils. The degree of modifications may vary but exclusion from the National Curriculum should never occur. That is the challenge for the special educator.'*

Ashdown *et al.*, 1991, pp. 17–18

This was a bold attitude, but can be seen as typical of the response which teachers in special schools have made in addressing the National Curriculum. Accepting that the needs of those pupils with the most challenging difficulties were ill considered in the conception of the National Curriculum, teachers have worked hard to adapt and modify curriculum content in order to make it more accessible. At the centre of debate for most schools has been the issue of balance. While acknowledging the importance of the National Curriculum, particularly as a link between what happens in the special school with what is taught in the mainstream, teachers of pupils with SEN have striven to achieve a model which can provide for the whole. This has often meant identifying opportunities for tackling a pupil's social or personal needs within the core and foundation subjects. It has also led to a debate about where the time may be found for the discrete teaching of skills and understanding that do not fall readily under the National Curriculum umbrella.

Byers (1999) in a review of the initiatives of teachers of pupils with severe and profound and multiple learning difficulties in curriculum development, recognises that issues of curriculum balance remain. He suggests that schools are unlikely to succeed in addressing this problem until a meaningful debate has been conducted regarding our current priorities and future aspirations for all pupils with severe or profound learning difficulties. He suggests that special schools have been in the vanguard of developments when it has come to examining the means by which the National Curriculum can be modified, adapted, and interpreted in order to provide access for pupils with a range of needs. In many respects this has been achieved by an analysis of the skills and understanding which pupils need to tackle the subject content of the core and foundation subjects. More importantly, it has involved teachers in an investigation of teaching approaches, which has ensured that the individual needs of pupils are recognised and addressed as effectively as those demands made by subject content.

Special schools have avoided the pitfalls of tokenism by developing planning and assessment approaches which recognise the value of providing experiences to pupils, alongside the recording of achievements. For example, Byers and others (Turner, 1998; Rose, 1998b) suggest that the National Curriculum may be conceived as a vehicle for developing important social, moral and personal understanding in children. Turner (1998) demonstrates how history has been used to promote an understanding of empathy, and the development of imagination in pupils with severe learning difficulties. Grove and Peacey (1999) suggest that mathematics specialists have taken a broad view in recognising that early perceptual experiences provide an important entry into their subject, and that teachers in special schools have become adept at enabling pupils to access such experiences through a range of strategies.

Elsewhere, Byers (1998) has demonstrated how the link between the requirements of the National Curriculum, and a prioritising of personal and social education needs can be achieved. He suggests that for teachers in special schools, the need to maintain a focus upon personal, social and health education remains a priority. A model of curriculum development is offered which shows how balance may be achieved through a synthesis of National Curriculum requirements and personal and social priorities. At the core of his argument is the establishment of a set of principles which places an equal value upon the development of ethos and learning processes, such as pupil involvement, to that given to curriculum content. He refers to the work of Buck and Inman (1995) who emphasise the role of education in the promotion of well-adjusted individuals through a focus on self-development. Their suggestion that all youngsters need to develop person attributes which include self-esteem, the ability to maintain effective interpersonal relationships within a moral framework, and to be self-aware, finds favour with teachers who have committed themselves to working with pupils with SEN. The task ahead for teachers is to ensure that a balanced curriculum provides the means by which these priorities may be addressed, while tackling the expectations of a curriculum laid down by statute.

5.4 The curriculum challenge for an inclusive future

This is the challenge confronting all teachers. How can this elusive goal of curriculum balance be achieved? Teachers in special schools have faced with fortitude and innovation many curriculum challenges. When the National Curriculum was introduced, despite calls in some quarters for special school teachers to reject it out of hand, modifications were made, and teaching approaches and resources developed which ensured that all pupils gained access to core and foundation subjects. In a review of the impact of the National Curriculum upon a sample of special schools, Halpin and Lewis (1996) discovered that headteachers were generally welcoming of the introduction of a common curriculum framework intended to embrace all pupils. The headteachers interviewed by these researchers cited increased expectation of academic performance and a broadening of curriculum opportunities provided to pupils with special needs, as positive aspects of the introduction of a National Curriculum. However, they also spoke of a tension between its introduction and the ability to maintain their focus upon individuality, and aspects of teaching which had traditionally addressed the personal, social and emotional needs of their pupils. It was clear from their data that the special schools in their survey had a desire to be a part of the National Curriculum but needed assistance in managing it in a way which would recognise the reasoning by which pupils had been placed in segregated provision. If the curriculum provided in special schools is not to differ from that provided in the mainstream, where is the justification for retaining special schools? After all, in terms of subject resources, a small special school cannot hope to compete with a large secondary school. The justification for the current retention of special schools must reside in their ability to provide an education which in complementing that of the mainstream recognises that pupils need a curriculum which does not merely mimic that provided by the ordinary school.

Successful inclusion will need to be built upon a curriculum model that embraces the whole range of pupil needs. In reflecting upon the changes which have taken place in the education of pupils with special educational needs since the publication of her 1978 report, Warnock (1999) has asserted that:

> 'my own view was, and is, that there is still a place for special
> schools, as centres of expertise. They are also a necessary part of the

education of some children, such as those who used to be called
"maladjusted" and the very severely multiply disabled.'   TES, 1999, p. 33

If we are to establish special schools as centres of expertise within a more inclusive educational system, a step towards the achievement of this may well reside within the curriculum structures that can be provided. The special school of the future will need to address the paradox of being a part of the mainstream of education while providing a service which is in some ways significantly different from it. This will require a re-appraisal of curriculum balance, asserting the rights of all pupils to have their individual needs more accurately assessed and addressed, alongside a recognition of their achievements.

In order to move towards a more comprehensive educational ideal which embraces special and mainstream schools in partnership, a number of important steps will need to be taken. LEAs, in line with the recommendations of the Green Paper (DfEE, 1997) must put into place formal arrangements for closer liaison between mainstream and special schools. If the focus of such arrangements remains purely at an administrative level, it will have minimal impact. However, the provision of opportunities for staff to establish a joint overview of all pupils with SEN within their institutions could lead to a more comprehensive and effective system of planning and management. Movement of both pupils and staff between schools would enable the best practices to be shared.

The current gulf between special and mainstream schools is unacceptable in an era that is concerned with equal opportunities and human rights. In the present situation some pupils in special schools are denied an opportunity to have their curriculum needs addressed with access to appropriate resources such as laboratories, workshops and gymnasia. Similar difficulties exist in providing for the needs of SEN pupils in mainstream schools. They are subjected to a curriculum which cannot hope to address specific aspects of their individual needs, and which fails to provide teaching approaches designed to consider learning styles different from those of the majority of their classmates. A more flexible system, encouraging movement between establishments, and providing a more analytical approach to addressing the needs of individuals would be welcomed by many teachers. Within the current model of provision there are too many occasions when we see pupils who suffer because of this lack of flexibility. For example, pupils with emotional and behavioural difficulties (EBD) who, often after a period of exclusion, find themselves attending a special school. Taken away from their peers, and labelled as having SEN, they are expected to develop positive attitudes to learning before being returned to the mainstream. Not surprisingly, the system fails many of these pupils, who either remain in the special school, or after returning to the mainstream find themselves excluded again. During their time in the special school these pupils are generally provided with a similar curriculum diet to that which they have found difficult in the school from which they have been excluded. Furthermore, the special school may be attempting to provide this curriculum with resources and facilities which are clearly inferior to those available in the mainstream. The pressure to conform to a mainstream school curriculum model does not afford the opportunities which are required to focus upon a need to promote a more positive attitude to learning in pupils, for whom the mainstream curriculum has come to represent a source of failure. The opportunity for such pupils to have their needs addressed through an approach which provides for time in more than one establishment on the basis of a careful analysis of curriculum needs could have many benefits. First, it could ensure that those aspects of a pupil's learning needs, which are not readily addressed within the limited structures imposed by a mainstream curriculum, could be recognised, planned for and addressed by staff from the special school. Second, it would enable the pupil to maintain the important social links with mainstream peers, and to continue working alongside those pupils in subjects which are seen as appropriate and in which progress can be maintained.

In curriculum terms, such an arrangement would require recognition of the important cusp between the mainstream and special provision. A special school curriculum that bears little resemblance to the mainstream is likely to become isolated and to deny opportunities for its pupils to become more included within society. Special schools will need to continue to develop and modify the National Curriculum in terms of both content and delivery. However, a special school which fails to recognise that the National Curriculum is only one element of a whole curriculum model will be doing a grave disservice to its population. A balanced curriculum will be one which, having identified the needs of its specific population, develops teaching approaches and curriculum content leading to improvements in all areas of pupils' needs. Schools which achieve this, while recognising the entitlement of pupils to gain access to their mainstream schools through shared common curriculum elements, will be providing a service not only to those pupils on the special school roll, but potentially to a number from the mainstream schools with whom they enter into partnership. Mainstream schools will look to special schools for support only when they feel confident that they can recognise the important curriculum overlap. If special schools are perceived as providing an education that is completely different from the mainstream, they will become further separated and will be denying opportunities to pupils who may benefit from a bilateral approach. However, if special schools are not identified as providing curriculum balance and offering new opportunities, they will cease to have a place within an integrated education system.

The demands placed upon special schools for such a change of approach will be great. Yet teachers in special schools have always risen to a challenge. The advantages to all are considerable. Special schools will need to continue to develop a curriculum that can cater for the needs of those pupils who provide the greatest challenge to our educational system. By ensuring that these pupils have access to peers who may be spending time in both mainstream and special provision, and by providing opportunities for shared curriculum access where appropriate, special schools will be playing an important role in addressing the aims of inclusion. Mainstream schools will need to become more effective in assessing the needs of their pupils, and must be encouraged to work closely with special schools.

Sebba *et al*. (1993) suggest that a whole curriculum model would recognise the individuality of pupils. In so doing, it would examine elements of the National Curriculum, a developmental curriculum and an additional curriculum which identified pupil needs in terms of their current and ongoing individual needs. Balance, they suggest, would be achieved when the needs of the pupil were considered in relation to each of these curricular elements. Little has happened in the intervening years to suggest that this premise has changed. Indeed, this model of whole curriculum development was seen as an important step in the promotion of a more inclusive education system. The need to work towards such a model remains and continues to be a critical factor if we are to achieve greater inclusion. It is clear that since the discussion of this whole curriculum model was given such prominence at the start of the 1990s, subsequent legislation has mitigated against its achievement. The dominance of National Curriculum assessment procedures, and a narrow concentration upon achievement in core subject areas, have resulted in a devaluing of those other aspects of the curriculum which could ensure balance for all pupils. As this has happened, teachers in special schools have come to question the National Curriculum and to consider whether those elements traditionally found within the developmental and additional curriculum have been devalued.

The time must surely have come for a whole system reappraisal of curriculum balance. The curriculum model currently provided in schools has become more exclusionary than was ever intended, and balance has been lost in the rush to raise standards in narrow academic terms. Teachers in special schools have developed a range of skills in identifying and planning for pupil individual needs, which could have major benefits to mainstream colleagues. Similarly, they have become adept in making the necessary modifications to the National Curriculum. While these teachers have endeavoured to respond to the requirements of curriculum legislation which has clearly failed to address the specific needs of their pupil population, teachers in the mainstream have become increasingly concerned for the small proportion of their pupils whose needs are not being adequately addressed. It is these pupils, and teachers charged with their responsibility, who have most to gain from revisiting a whole curriculum model, and from sharing in a closer professional partnership.

5.5   The ultimate goal

The future development of special schools is an issue for the education establishment as a whole. The naïvety of administrators who believe that one model of curricular provision based solely upon mainstream schools can meet the needs of all pupils must be challenged. The ultimate goal might be to realign the schooling system to enable all schools to have the flexibility to cater for the entire school population. As educators we should be striving to achieve this end. However, such a goal will need to be gained by building upon our current expertise in working with pupils with special educational needs. Teachers in special schools have committed themselves to providing learning opportunities, and approaches which have focused specifically upon the needs of pupils. At present this is, to an extent, at odds with an interpretation of curriculum purpose that is out of alignment with the original concept of a curriculum for all. A truly comprehensive curriculum recognises the needs of all pupils within the education system, and provides teachers with the opportunity to plan to meet those needs by making use of the expertise available in both mainstream and special schools.

References

Ashdown, R., Carpenter, B. and Bovair, K. *The Curriculum Challenge*, London, Falmer, 1991.

Booth, T., Ainscow, M. and Dyson, A. 'Understanding inclusion and exclusion in the English competitive education system', *International Journal of Inclusive Education* 1 (4), 1997, pp. 337–55.

Buck, M. and Inman, S. *Adding Value? Schools' Responsibility for Pupils' Personal Development*, Stoke-on-Trent, Trentham Books, 1995.

Byers, R. 'Personal and social development for pupils with learning difficulties', in *Promoting Inclusive Practice*, C. Tilstone, L. Florian and R. Rose, London, Routledge, 1998.

Byers, R. 'Experience and achievement: initiatives in curriculum development for pupils with severe and profound and multiple learning difficulties', *British Journal of Special Education* 26 (4), 1999, pp. 184–8.

Carpenter, B., Ashdown. R. and Bovair, K. *Enabling Access*, London, David Fulton, 1996.

Department for Education and Employment *Excellence for All Children: Meeting Special Educational Needs*, London, The Stationery Office, 1997.

Dyson, A. 'Inclusion and inclusions: theories and discourses in inclusive education', in *World Yearbook of Education: Inclusive Education*, H. Daniels, and P. Garner (eds), London, Kogan Page, 1999.

Farrell, P. 'The integration of children with severe learning difficulties: a review of the recent literature', *Journal of Applied Research in Intellectual Disabilities* 10 (1), 1997, pp.1–14.

Feiler, A. and Gibson, H. 'Threats to the inclusive movement', *British Journal of Special Education* 26 (3), 1999, pp. 147–51.

Foucault, M. *Madness and Civilization*, London, Routledge, 1997.

Fuchs, D. and Fuchs, L.S. 'Inclusive schools movement and the radicalization of special education reform', *Exceptional Children* 60 (4), 1994, pp. 294–309.

Grove, N. and Peacey, N. 'Teaching subjects to pupils with profound and multiple learning difficulties', *British Journal of Special Education* 26 (2), 1999, pp. 83–6.

Halpin, D. and Lewis, A. 'The impact of the National Curriculum on twelve schools in England', *European Journal of Special Needs Education* 11 (1), 1996, pp. 95–105.

Hornby, G. 'Inclusion or delusion: can one size fit all?', *Support for Learning* 14 (4), 1999, pp. 152–7.

Jenkinson, J. *Mainstream or Special?*, London, Routledge, 1997.

Lieberman, L.M. 'Preserving special education .... for those who need it', in *Controversial Issues Confronting Special Education*, W. Stainback and S. Stainback (eds), Boston, Allyn and Bacon, 1992.

Logan, K.R. and Malone, D.M 'Comparing instructional contexts of students with and without severe disabilities in general education classrooms', *Exceptional Children* 64 (3), 1998, pp. 343–58.

Mithaug, D.E. 'The alternative to ideological inclusion', in *Inclusive Schooling*, S.J. Vitello and D.E. Mithaug, Mahwah, NJ, Lawrence Erlbaum, 1998.

NCC (National Curriculum Council) *Curriculum Guidance 3: The Whole Curriculum*, York, NCC, 1990.

Oliver, M. 'The social and political context of educational policy: the case for special needs', in *The Politics of Special Educational Needs,* L. Barton (ed.), London, Falmer, 1988.

Paul, P.V. and Ward, M.E. 'Inclusion paradigms in conflict', *Theory into Practice* 35 (1), 1996, pp. 4–11.

Rieser, R. 'Disabled history or a history of the disabled', in *Disability Equality in the Classroom: A Human Rights Issue*, R. Rieser and M. Mason (eds) London, ILEA (Inner London Education Authority), 1990.

Rose, R. 'Including pupils: developing a partnership in learning', in *Promoting Inclusive Practice*, C. Tilstone, L. Florian and R. Rose, (eds), London, Routledge, 1998a.

Rose, R. 'The curriculum: a vehicle for inclusion or a lever for exclusion?', in *Promoting Inclusive Practice*, C. Tilstone, L. Florian and R. Rose, (eds), London, Routledge, 1998b.

Rose, R., Fergusson, A., Coles, C., Byers, R. and Banes, D. *Implementing the Whole Curriculum for Pupils with Learning Difficulties*, London, David Fulton, 1994.

Sebba, J., Byers, R. and Rose, R. *Redefining the Whole Curriculum for Pupils with Learning Difficulties*, London, David Fulton, 1993.

Söder, M. 'A research perspective on integration', in *Inclusive Education: A Global Agenda*, S.J. Pijl, C.J.W. Meijer and S. Hegarty, (eds), London, Routledge, 1997.

Turner, A. 'It would have been bad: the development of historical imagination and empathy in a group of secondary aged pupils with severe learning difficulties', *British Journal of Special Education* 25 (4), 1998, pp. 164–7.

Warnock, M. 'If only we had known then ...' *Times Educational Supplement* (Millennium Edition), 31 December, London, TES, 1999.

Jean B. Crockett

6.1 Introduction

American education is a-buzz with concerns of accountability for the
learning of all students but befuddled about what actually constitutes
appropriate curriculum and *appropriate assessment*. Let me illustrate this
predicament by recalling a recent cover of the *New Yorker* magazine that
portrays a concert stage, empty except for a tiny figure in a black tuxedo
timidly making his way toward an imposing grand piano. As I looked at the
picture, I wondered, 'what is he going to play, and how is he going to play
it?' To me, the illustration epitomises the challenges of high-stakes
accountability. These questions came to my mind: When can Frederick
Chopin's Opus 64, Number 1: 'The Minute Waltz', be played in 90 seconds?
Who decides whether the pianist will play from an enlarged print version
of the original score or from the big note 'easy piano' version? Which
alterations accommodate the player and which ones modify the music?
When it comes to playing this standard from the classical repertoire, just
what are we asking this particular performer to do and what do we expect
of him? What were the instructional goals for his performance: keyboard
speed and romantic interpretation? Or was he trained in mastery of the 'on'
switch so the electronic piano could automatically play flawless Chopin in
60 seconds flat? We can no longer take classic expectations for granted
when the technical virtuosity of electronics makes beautiful music despite
the limitations of the performer.

My perspective with regard to curriculum, instruction, and accountability
for results in special education has been informed through my association
with technology-dependent students and with Dr Henry Viscardi. An
advisor on issues of vocational rehabilitation to seven US presidents,
Viscardi was born in 1912 and walks with the aid of prosthetic limbs. He is
fond of saying that most of us are ordinary people seeking extraordinary
destinies, but that persons with disabilities are extraordinary people
seeking ordinary destinies. Viscardi's perspective enjoins us to confront, not
merely to celebrate, individual differences by providing beneficial
opportunities for children that inhibit their disabilities from handicapping
their futures.

6.2 The business of prevention

I agree with those who suggest that the curriculum of preventing handicaps from developing in children with disabilities cannot always be employed in the regular classroom with the use of the general education curriculum (Crockett and Kauffman, 1999; Hornby *et al.*, 1997; Keogh and Speece, 1996; Zigmond, 1995, 2000). Laurence Lieberman (in Crockett and Kauffman, 1999) speaks clearly to this point, defining for whom special education was initially intended in the United States and suggesting that understanding special education beyond inclusion comes from making the distinction between a disability and handicap. Not everyone with a disability is handicapped, says Lieberman. Handicaps exist when disabilities get in the way of life choices:

> *'Special education is for people with disabilities who are in danger of becoming handicapped if they do not receive special services. Why do specialists provide orientation and mobility training for blind children, sometimes in special settings? Because they are trying to prevent the handicap of not being able to move in space from developing in a disabled person. Why do we pull students with learning disabilities out of class? We are trying to prevent the handicap of not being able to read from developing in a disabled child. That is why we do special education. We are trying to prevent handicaps from developing in students with disabilities .... Special education is not for regular education curriculum failures. Special education is for individuals with disabilities.'*

Lieberman in Crockett and Kauffman, 1999, pp. 163–4

Lieberman's words suggest that special education is in the business of prevention – in this case, preventing disabilities from handicapping the futures of our children.

Kauffman (1999, p. 448) notes that although 'prevention seems to be everyone's rhetorical darling', most of our talk about prevention lacks substance or conviction. While we agree that taking preventive action is a good idea, we so readily displace goals for the future with responses to problems of immediate consequence. We lose our vision and cannot see the forest for the trees. In designing service delivery systems, special educators easily run the risk of 'preventing prevention.' Afraid that our students might be left out of educational reform, and left behind in this era of accountability, it is easy for us to get confused about what we intend to prevent in the first place. Are we preventing our students from being left behind or are we preventing our students from getting ahead? Perhaps the answer to both questions is this: it depends. It is helpful to question the presumptions that underpin regular programming and accountability. We can return to the roots of special education to probe what we know about individual consideration in curriculum, instruction, and assessment to better ground our thinking.

6.3 Foundational framework for special education

The following framework is presented to inform this discussion of outcomes-based education for students with SEN. This framework is intended to assist decision-makers in designing appropriate programming by clarifying five core principles of special education practice (Crockett, 1999):

◆ providing *universal educational access and accountability* for all students;
◆ ensuring *individual consideration* for each student whose exceptional learning characteristics require an extraordinary response;
◆ addressing the *appropriate educational benefit* of each student with special needs through equitable public policies;
◆ ensuring *effective programming* that demonstrably improves academic, social, and behavioural outcomes;
◆ establishing *productive partnerships* between students, parents, professionals, and communities that foster high expectations, support research-based strategies, and target positive results for exceptional learners.

Figure 6.1 illustrates how these principles are sequenced and build upon one another.

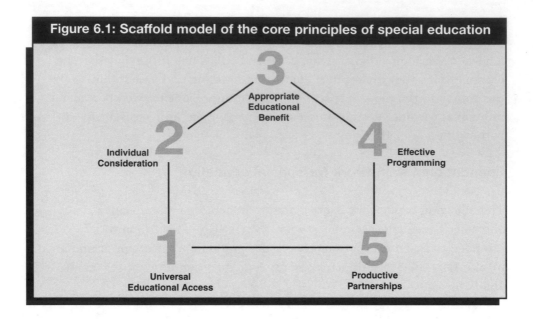

Figure 6.1: Scaffold model of the core principles of special education

Figure 6.2 renders a heuristic impression of the core principles illustrating their sequential iteration around the outside of the figure, and their dynamic interaction with one another across the pentagon. In addition to illustrating the linkages between and across the five core principles, this pentagon model (adapted from Hutchins, 1993) is intended to serve as a mnemonic device helping practitioners to conceptualise the core foundations of special education.

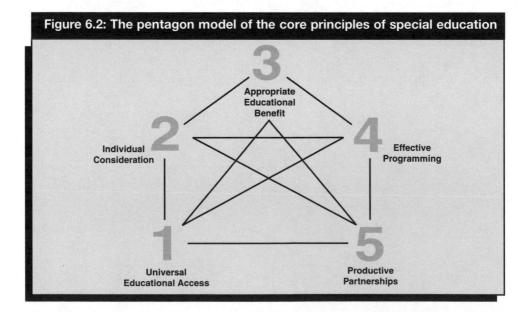

Figure 6.2: The pentagon model of the core principles of special education

6.4 Probing presumptions

My intention is to use special education's conceptual core as a guide to probing the presumptions that underpin accountability for higher outcomes, and inclusive participation and progress in the general curriculum for students with SEN. My goal is to reveal these presumptions for what they are: *rebuttable* presumptions that stand in the service of a free and individually appropriate public education. American policy calls this by the acronym FAPE. In special education, rebuttable presumptions are universal prescriptions that are assumed innocent until proven guilty of not addressing the educational benefit of vulnerable students. For exceptional learners who often require different resources to achieve different results, presumptions can cause harm unless we have the data and the drive to rebut them when necessary. I will examine some of what we know about ensuring meaningful educational access, effective programming, and better outcomes for students with disabilities. I will rely on data gathered from the multiple perspectives of parents, public policies, and educational professionals to demonstrate that even rebuttable presumptions are not always benign educational strategies.

6.4.1 Providing universal educational access and accountability

Stake remarks that '*as education in America has passed from teacher-driven recitation to government-driven accountability, the role of formal assessment has grown .... In the last 30 years, formalised student assessment has become the most widely used indicator of school quality*'. Martha Thurlow states that forty of America's fifty states have formal systems of accountability where schools as well as their teachers and administrators face negative consequences for poor results in student achievement on wide-scale tests (Thurlow and McLaughlin, 1999).

1999, p. 669

6.4.2 Presumptions about accountability

The strong emphasis on standards-based accountability paired with heavy consequences for failure has made for good press with news stories cautioning parents and satirising punitive policies. While political pressure for higher performance has engendered scams and satire, it has also raised valid questions about what we should be looking for in holding special education students accountable. In recent years, frameworks for identifying student outcomes have been advanced, as well as practical strategies for designing curriculum and targeting instruction (Kameenui and Carnine, 1998). In considering these frameworks and strategies, it is imperative to tease out the political capital associated with accountability from the substantive gains to be made from identifying student outcomes and targeting their achievement.

6.4.3 Political accountability

Accountability has been defined as *'evidence that schools are doing what they are supposed to be doing'* (Thurlow *et al.*, 1998) and in standards-based reform, that translates into evidence by results: Have students learned what the public wants them to know? Can they read? Can they solve problems? Can they demonstrate these skills on assessments that test their competence? Several premises characterise the standards-based approach to educational reform: (1) standards will be set at a high level; and (2) these high standards will apply to all students (McDonnell *et al.*, 1997).

With regard to special education, however, there are cautions surrounding standards-based reforms (CEC, 1992). For instance, standard-setting is arbitrary; there is no empirical evidence that indicates *what* students should know and by *when* they should know it. Standard-setting groups are not required to consider students with diverse needs and sometimes they set standards in core subject areas only. This results in narrowing the valued curriculum when we know that some students thrive on the challenge of alternative curricula.

6.4.4 Student accountability

Although goal setting and the monitoring of achievement are familiar practices to special educators, efficiently linking individualised programming and the general curriculum with assessment of students' proficiency in that curriculum currently exceeds the technologies of both pedagogy and accountability. Special educators still face thoughtful questions:

◆ What do we want students to know and be able to do?
◆ What kinds of learning experiences produce these outcomes?
◆ What does it take to transform schools into places where student outcomes are enhanced?
◆ How will we know if we are successful? What kinds of accountability are needed to ensure a positive relationship between our services and interventions and student outcomes and other desired results? (Schrag, cited in Ysseldyke *et al.*, 1992)

Critical thought should also be given to how the information generated from political accountability systems will be used with regard to exceptional learners. Stake points out the gap between the realities of standardised wide-scale assessments and conventional assumptions of their usefulness:

> *'The presumptions that assessments indicate the quality of teaching, the appropriateness of curricula, and the progress of the reform movement – commonplace presumptions in politics and the media – are unwarranted. Proper validation research would tell us the strength or weakness of our conclusions about student accomplishment. But those studies have not been commissioned.'*

Stake, 1999, p. 669

Stake calls for the research community to provide better descriptions and better evidence of the consequences of assessments to rebut the presumption that legislated assessment positively changes instruction – especially for *'the least privileged families and the most vulnerable children'* (ibid., p. 672). Real advances for these students may depend on *'putting more investment in ipsative (person-referenced) assessment and giving less credence to normative (norm-referenced) assessment'* (ibid., p. 672). Because in his view, *'few teachers know how to respond to poor student performance, other than to try harder'* (ibid., p. 670), one of the consequences of high-stakes testing is to manipulate school and class rosters to excuse low-scoring children from participation. The most common ways of purifying the testing pool at present appear to be inappropriate classification of 'special education' students, and inappropriate retention in a lower grade level of those students who might sink the school's scores were they to be promoted with their classmates. With regard to systems level accountability, Stake urges caution:

> *'Holding schools accountable is in no way dependent on having each child tied to a core curriculum and tested on the same items. A single test for all may be cheaper, but it is not a service to a diverse society.'*

1999, p. 670

Despite the political rhetoric, little attention has been given to researching the effects of the politically popular issue of standards-based reforms either for students with or without disabilities (McDonnell *et al.*, 1997). With regard to the political cachet attached to systems accountability and social inclusion for students with SEN, Cook *et al.* (1997, p.136) ask: *'Is the attractive ideal of academic excellence for all more than idealistic whimsy or idle banter to enhance the political acceptability of either reform?'*

6.4.5 Presumptions about access to the general curriculum

The provisions of the 1997 Individuals with Disabilities Education Act (IDEA) and its regulations presume that exceptional learners have gained educational access; consequently, the new amendments target educational results. In response, the US Department of Education has set three outcome-based goals designed to improve state special education programs by providing access to high-quality education, challenging standards, and preparation for employment and independent living (US Department of Education, 1998). The following summary underscores the department's presumptive view of the 'general curriculum' as playing a crucial role in meeting the requirements for accountability embedded in the Act. There is strong emphasis on the following elements:

◆ monitoring student performance by including all students in regular state assessments or alternate assessments;
◆ including all children with disabilities in the general education curriculum to the maximum extent appropriate and measuring their participation and progress in that curriculum by the increased time they spend in regular classrooms;
◆ providing students 14 years and older with appropriate services to encourage school completion and future employment, and to facilitate their transition from school to work or post-secondary education.

These policies endorsing curricular inclusion and accountability rely on the presumption that more children will be successful than we think if they are included in and tested on their competence in the general education curriculum. Judith Heumann, Director of the US Office of Special Education and Rehabilitation Services (1999) states that students with disabilities have not fully participated in state and district assessments and thus have been short-changed by the low expectations and less challenging curriculum that may result from exclusion. Heumann's remarks reveal further presumptions including that the general education curriculum is challenging and that alternative curricula and classrooms are *de facto* less challenging – without considering for whom they are less challenging and under what circumstances they are less challenging.

6.4.6 The challenges of universal educational access and accountability

While there is praise for measuring the educational progress of students with disabilities, there are concerns among American teachers and administrators about confusing the ethics of ensuring educational access and accountability with providing effective programming that is reasonably calculated to provide individual students with educational benefit. These practitioners are suspicious that this linkage serves the political agenda of equalising access for *all* students to the *same* high standards and the *same* curricular offerings without stopping to consider that access to these standards might not help *some* students to achieve meaningful outcomes at all.

With regard to preventing disabilities from handicapping the futures of our children, standards-based reforms raise three essential questions to consider in providing outcomes-based education for students with SEN:

1 How can we encourage the general public as well as members of our own school communities to hold high expectations for students with SEN?
2 How can we ensure appropriate programming and valid accountability systems that account for our students' progress, but also account for their differences?
3 How can we encourage our teachers to use curricular designs and instructional strategies, with proven track records of success, in addressing better outcomes for each of our students?

6.5 Challenging the presumptions by returning to the roots of special education

At a recent conference sponsored by the US Department of Education, a panel of three educators challenged presumptions about providing access to the general education curriculum and holding students with SEN accountable for progress within it. Each panel member could be called a pioneer, having shaped the field of contemporary American special education and the development of the federal law, the Individuals with Disabilities Education Act (IDEA), itself. Their perspectives bring insight to these essential questions.

Frank Boe: Individual consideration

Frank Boe, is a professor of special education. He is also deaf. He challenged the audience to consider what access means for contemporary special education students. Boe noted that access to educational programmes is still an issue in early intervention where too many children with disabilities, from birth to age three, are not receiving services at all. The pressing issue for school-aged youth, however, is not access to the general curriculum, but expectations for making the general education curriculum accessible to students who require extraordinary approaches to derive its benefits. Dr Boe spoke of his early schooling and recounted that he was fully included in general education classes but never received the specialised support that allowed him to have meaningful access to learning. He pointed out that although he had full access to the regular curriculum for twelve years, he did not begin to benefit from his education until he was 14 years old. It took him until high school to master the English language enough to gain information from what he read. Boe emphasised that access to the general curriculum for deaf students is different and defies conventional assumptions and expectations for accessibility. Genuine access to the general curriculum hinges on giving individual consideration to a student's unique learning characteristics so that specialised instruction can actually make the curriculum accessible to him or her.

Ed Martin: Educational benefit

Edwin W. Martin served as the Assistant US Secretary for Education when the Education for All Handicapped Children's Act (EAHCA) was enacted in 1975. He contrasted the individualised nature of special education with the differing premise in general education of a 'moulded general curriculum'. Martin expressed concerns that for special education students 'access to the general curriculum is a flawed concept' because it postulates a goal before considering programming that might be more appropriate in meeting the needs of an individual student. Dr Martin stated that we must value individual programming that addresses appropriate outcomes for special education students and be aware of our fundamental assumption. He emphasised that *we need data on student outcomes* to guide our programming decisions.

Fred Weintraub: Effective programming

Frederick J. Weintraub directed public policy for CEC for thirty years and was one of the group who helped to write the original legislation that became the IDEA. Weintraub remarked that special education proceeds from an underlying assumption: '*Special education exists in a curricular context.*' He stated that effective programming requires specialised instruction based on a child's unique educational needs, not simply aids and supplementary services. Weintraub, recalling his participation in developing the IDEA's requirement for individualised education plans (IEPs), emphasised the parallel requirement for teachers to set 'individualised *instructional* objectives' that were in accordance with the expectations of state education agencies. Weintraub acknowledged that, over time, IEP documents have lost their instructional focus, become prescriptions for narrow personal goals and low expectations, and have strayed from the underlying assumption of curricular context: '*Individualised within a larger context was the intent, not individualised in a vacuum.*' For Weintraub, effective programming based on beneficial curricula is preferable to the presumption that special education students will participate and progress in the general curriculum.

In challenging the conventional assumptions of universal participation and progress in the general education curriculum for students with disabilities, Boe, Martin and Weintraub grounded their remarks in the core principles of special education.

6.5.1 The least restrictive environment

Believing that current practices are best understood by anchoring them in an understanding of the past, James M. Kauffman and I (1999) took the notions of curricular and classroom inclusion back to the roots of special education to examine the policy tool known as 'the least restrictive environment', (LRE). We sought historical and contemporary evidence from parents, courts and classrooms to explore the notion of access to a meaningful educational opportunity. We found that parents of students with SEN, along with judges and educators, recommend that the practice of inclusion calls for a closer look to prevent children, whose exceptional learning needs require 'an extraordinary response' (cf. Kauffman, 1997), from falling through the cracks.

6.5.2 Parental concerns

With regard to accessibility and individual consideration, we found that parents of students with disabilities, past and present, seek social acceptance and full participation for their children in schools that offer them a *meaningful* opportunity to learn. Although total exclusion from education is no longer the threat, we found that not all parents of children with disabilities view regular classrooms as having the capacity to provide meaningful opportunities to learn, despite the best intentions of prescribed supplementary aids and services. Given the children's wide range of individual needs, the expectation that parents will embrace inclusive programming is often an oversimplified prediction of their preference. Karen Silver, the parent of a daughter severely affected by cerebral palsy, cautions:

> *'Not all children who require special education are the same. The diversity of programs which exist today came about because parents and educators fought for them, recognising that there was no single setting which could possibly meet the wide-ranging needs of the disabled school-age population.'*

Crockett and
Kauffman, 1999,
p. 184

6.5.3 Curricular expectations

In the early 1990s, position papers addressing the concept of 'full inclusion' were prepared by advocacy organisations representing parents, professionals, and persons with various disabilities. Advocates for The Association for Persons with Severe Handicaps (TASH) hailed inclusive education as '*a new way of thinking that embraces a sociology of acceptance of* all *children into the school community as active, fully participating members*' (TASH, 1993). Other groups, representing diverse learners, questioned general education's capacity to differentiate curricular, instructional, and behavioural approaches for *all* students. These statements called for appropriate educational access and accountability, not with visionary zeal, but with a realistic view towards preventing disabilities from remaining unaddressed and consequently handicapping life choices. These conflicting expectations for what constitutes a meaningful education for children with diverse learning needs influenced the preservation of the continuum of alternative placements and the individualised principles of placement in the LRE in the 1997 amendments to the IDEA. The statute is not insensitive to parental perspectives and now calls for the participation of parents in any decisions related to their child's special education (Crockett, 1999).

6.6 Addressing educational benefits

In studying the roots of special education, we found that the IEP process is considered by most stakeholders to be the heart and soul of the IDEA, essential to the formulation of appropriate programming for each child. Consequently, creating meaningful educational programmes, with individualised goals and objectives, and using them to guide instructional decisions continues to be integral to special education. As the law suggests, only when such a programme is designed, with collaborative and knowledgeable input from persons who know that child best, can appropriate instruction follow.

With regard to the legal obligation to provide educational benefit to children with disabilities, we found that the LRE, or the least restrictive appropriate placement, continues to be considered as a sub-set of *appropriateness*, or one element in providing an individual student with beneficial outcomes. There is deep confusion, however, over what is meant by the term 'least restrictive' as it is used in the language of special education. For example, from a sociological perspective, the word restrictive is synonymous with segregated so that the 'least restrictive' environment, for example, becomes the 'least segregated' environment, or the environment in which children with disabilities are least separated from their non-disabled peers (Villa and Thousand, 1995). From an educational perspective focused on increased accountability for results, the term 'least restrictive' implies an eco-behavioural interaction among an individual student, a prescribed educational programme, and an instructional setting calculated to provide him or her with academic and social benefit that includes non-disabled peers to the maximum extent appropriate for that student.

For decision-makers, problems occur when there is confusion about what a learning environment is handicapping in the first place – educational opportunity or social integration. Legally, the least restrictive alternative does not describe an inclusive curriculum or classroom location, but a procedural process in which a greater weight is given to the standard of individual appropriateness than to inclusion in the standard fare.

6.6.1 Rebuttable presumptions

Turnbull (1990, p.148) describes the LRE concept as a means by which to balance the values surrounding the provision of an *appropriate education (the student's right to and need for an appropriate education) with the values of individual rights of association*'. The concept of LRE, operationalised in schools as mainstreaming or inclusion, is not an immutable rule, but a rebuttable presumption favouring integration and common treatment, but allowing separation and deferential treatment (Turnbull, 1990). Rebuttable presumptions are often viewed as positive policy tools that offer affected parties greater protection from having no alternative to what they perceive as harmful. Determining what constitutes a suitable rebuttal, however, can be both ambiguous and complex. Martin suggests that the key to reducing ambiguity and increasing understanding lies in demonstrating what is meant by appropriate in that it is not empirically derived by student outcomes. 'Without data,' he says, 'all we have are assumptions.'

With regard to accountability for far-sighted programming, we found that most educators embrace greater participation and progress for students with disabilities in the educational mainstream. What these teachers fear is the prevention of their students' post-school success unless they are provided with appropriate curriculum and instruction, supportive peer and teacher interactions, and suitable organisation and management of their educational environments (Crockett and Kauffman, 1999).

Inadequate approaches to the instructional inclusion of students with disabilities threaten to marginalise special education from the centre of school reform, which emphasises, not downplays, the importance of academic curricula and accountability. Instructional practices flow from curricular imperatives dictating policies of class grouping, grade levels, grading practices, grade retention, and academic content (Crockett and Kauffman, 1998). *'Many students do not have the ability to keep pace with the curriculum the way it is structured within the general education classroom and thus may experience a different kind of segregation – the exclusion from the basic right to learn.'* The assumption that the general education curriculum is appropriate for students with disabilities begs critical questions: Can the curriculum be modified to meet the needs of all students? Can professional training positively affect teaching practice? Is it probable that all teachers will provide specialised instruction for individual students with disabilities as they attempt to provide personalised and

Schumm *et al.*, 1995, p. 335

accommodating educational experience for all students? Such questions have practical merit to school systems. If an accommodating general education provides academic and social benefit to a student so that he or she makes progress from grade to grade, then conceivably more students could be disenfranchised from mandated services, and more districts released from costly obligations (Zigmond, 1995).

6.7 What do we know about outcomes for special education students?

In planning the education of students with SEN beyond inclusion, several researchers suggest that we begin with the end in mind. Hornby (1999, p.125) targets inclusion in the community after students have left school *'as the actual end that educators are seeking. Inclusion in mainstream school may be a means to that end but is not the end itself.'* Hornby suggests that accessing high quality instruction that leads to a successful post-school life relies less on an obsession with curricular or classroom inclusion for students with SEN and more on providing a diversity of settings, strategies, and curricular options responsive to their diverse needs and strengths.

The results of Hocutt's (1996) investigation of various programme models that contribute to positive outcomes for exceptional learners supports Hornby's focus on diversification. Unfortunately, she found that *'no intervention has been designed that eliminates the impact of having a disability. With few exceptions, students with disabilities have not achieved commensurately with their non-disabled peers.'* It is clear from her study, however, that students' academic and social success is primarily affected by the instructional models employed and the classroom environment rather than by placement in general or special education settings. The most effective interventions for students with disabilities relied on intensive, individualised instruction with careful and frequent monitoring of student progress. These approaches were hard to find in typical classrooms. They required considerable investments of money, time, effort, and extensive support and training for teachers.

1996, p. 77

6.8 What do we know about effective programming?

Each of us has probably worked with children, disabled or not, who have struggled to keep up with their same-aged peers. Regardless of the terminology used to identify these children or the characteristics that describe their behaviours, they share the common denominator of school failure (Kameenui, 1993). *'More specifically, they are failing to achieve from traditional curriculum and instruction'* (Simmons and Kameenui, 1996). High quality instruction relies on more than an inclusive philosophy; it depends on pedagogical prowess. Kameenui and Carnine (1998) suggest that providing high quality instruction may become increasingly difficult as our educational resources shrink and the diversity of our students' learning and curricular needs increase. Developing effective pedagogical strategies that help teachers organise and present information in a memorable, manageable and meaningful way to students requires careful analysis of what we want students to be able to do and understand. This approach presumes that teachers respond to the characteristics of diverse learners that have the highest causal connection with academic failure: learning difficulties that are rooted in the areas of language. They also suggest that while teachers might not have control over the devastating social problems of family breakdown, poverty, violence and crime, they can *'assert a great deal of control over what occurs in the classroom. They will need to if students are to acquire the knowledge needed'* to meet the challenges of the twenty-first century.

1998, p. 41

6.9   Conclusion

This discussion of accountability and curriculum began by examining the presumption of providing students with disabilities both to participate and progress in the general education curriculum. It has made its way through state and local levels of policy-making into the classroom where pedagogical decision-making holds the greatest promise of doing two things – rebutting presumptions that just don't fit, and preventing failure for students who are falling behind.

As special educators, we can draw on the roots of our field to help us further productive partnerships with parents and professional colleagues that utilise a diversity of research-based strategies and target success for exceptional learners. All of us together can prevent disabilities from handicapping the futures of our children when we use a variety of reliable approaches that mitigate their learning difficulties, and support their academic and social success with high expectations. In this way, to paraphrase Dr Henry Viscardi's words, we just might have the chance to help some extraordinary people seek – and find – ordinary destinies.

References

Boe, F., Martin, E. and Weintraub, F. *Access: Defining the Construct Historically, Legally, and Politically*, Plenary session panel discussion at the OSEP Research Project Directors' Conference, 16 July, Washington, DC, 1996.

Cook, B.G., Gerber, M.M. and Semmel, M.I. 'Reflections on "Are effective schools reforms effective for all students?" The implications of joint outcome production for school reform', *Exceptionality* 7, 1997, pp. 131–7.

Council for Exceptional Children. *Statement Prepared for Testimony before the House Subcommittee on Elementary, Secondary, and Vocational Education*, Reston, VA, Author, 1992.

Crockett, J.B. 'Viable alternatives for students with disabilities: exploring the origins and interpretations of the LRE', *Exceptionality* 8, 1999, pp. 43–60.

Crockett, J.B. and Kauffman, J.M. 'Classrooms for students with learning disabilities: realities, dilemmas, and recommendations for service delivery', in *Learning about Learning Disabilities*, B. Wong (ed.), San Diego, CA, Academic Press, 1998.

Crockett, J.B. and Kauffman, J.M. *The Least Restrictive Environment: Its Origins and Interpretations in Special Education*, Mahwah, NJ, Lawrence Erlbaum, 1999.

Heumann, J. 'Alternate assessments: accounting for students with the most severe disabilities', *The Special Educator* 14 (12), 1999, pp. 1–4.

Hocutt, A. M. 'Effectiveness of special education: is placement the critical factor?', *The Future of Children, Special Education for Students with Disabilties* 6 (1), 1996, pp. 77–102.

Hornby, G. 'Inclusion, exclusion, and confusion', *Liberty* 4 (6), 1999, pp. 121–5.

Hornby, G., Atkinson, M. and Howard, J. *Controversial Issues in Special Education*, London, David Fulton, 1997.

Hutchins, D.E. 'The group pentagon: designing highly effective brief groups', unpublished manuscript, Virginia Tech, Blacksburg, 1993.

Kameenui, E.J. 'Diverse learners and the tyranny of time: don't fix blame; fix the leaky roof', *Reading Teacher* 46, 1993, pp. 376–83.

Kameenui, E.J. and Carnine, D.W. *Effective Teaching Strategies that Accommodate Diverse Learners*. Upper Saddle River, NJ, Merrill, 1998.

Kauffman, J.M. 'Caricature, science, and exceptionality', *Remedial and Special Education* 18, 1997, pp. 130–2.

Kauffman, J.M. 'How we prevent the prevention of emotional and behavioral disorders', *Exceptional Children* 65, 1999, pp. 448–68.

Keogh, B.K. and Speece, D. 'Learning disabilities within the context of schooling', in D. Speece and B.K. Keogh (eds) *Research on Classroom Ecologies: Implications for inclusion of children with learning disabilities*, Mahwah, NJ, Lawrence Erlbaum, 1996.

Martin, E.W. 'Case studies on inclusion: worst fears realised', *Journal of Special Education* 29 (2), 1995, pp. 192–9.

McDonnell, L.M., McLaughlin, M.J. and Morison, P. (eds) *Educating One and All: Students with Disabilities and Standards-Based-Reform*. Washington, DC, National Academy Press, 1997.

Schumm, J.S., Vaughn, S., Haager, D., McDowell, J., Rothlein, L. and Saumell, L. 'General education teacher planning: what can students with learning disabilities expect?', *Exceptional Children* 61, 1995, pp. 335–52.

Simmons, D.C. and Kameenui, E.J. 'A focus on curriculum design: when children fail', *Focus on Exceptional Children* 28 (7), 1996, pp. 1–16.

Stake, R. 'The goods on American education', *Phi Delta Kappan* 80, 1999, pp. 668–72.

The Association for Persons with Severe Handicaps (TASH) *Resolution on Inclusive Education,* Baltimore, TASH, 1993.

Thurlow, M. and McLaughlin, M. *Accountability for Student Outcomes: Is this enough?*, paper presented at OSEP Research Project Directors' Conference, 15 July, Washington, DC, 1999.

Thurlow, M.L., Elliott, J.L. and Ysseldyke, J.E. *Testing Students with Disabilities: Practical Strategies for Complying with District and State Requirements*, Thousand Oaks, CA, Corwin, 1998.

Turnbull, H.R. *Free Appropriate Public Education: The Law and Children with Disabilities*, Denver, CO, Love Publishing Company, 1990.

US Department of Education *Twentieth Annual Report to Congress on the Implementation of the Individuals with Disabilities Education Act*, Washington, DC, Office of Special Education Programs, US Government Printing Office, 1998.

Villa, R.A. and Thousand, J.S. *Creating an Inclusive School*, Alexandria, VA, Association for Supervision and Curriculum Development, 1995.

Ysseldyke, J.E., Thurlow, M.L. and Shriner, J.G. 'Outcomes are for special educators too', *Teaching Exceptional Children*, 25 (1) 1992, pp 36–50.

Zigmond, N. 'An exploration of the meaning and practice of special education in the context of full inclusion of students with learning disabilities', *The Journal of Special Education* 29, 1995, pp. 109–15.

Zigmond, N. 'Reflections on a research career: research as detective work', *Exceptional Children* 66, 2000, pp. 295–304.

Chapter 7 —

Is a social model sufficient to enable
inclusive educational practice?

Mike Blamires

7.1   Introduction

This chapter compares the three dominant educational models that address concerns traditionally lying within the areas of difficulty, disaffection and disability. In doing so the potential and limitations of each model will be explored. Allan (1999) has suggested that 'Foucault's toolbox' for analysis has been under-utilised within this area of education. Therefore this chapter also attempts to apply these 'tools' in order to test their utility in casting light upon the differences between each model. To begin the comparison between these models of practice, a number of headings are utilised to highlight the different aspect and values of the each paradigm. These are presented within Tables 7.1 and 7.2 with subsequent discussion. From this I suggest that the social model is necessary but not sufficient to enable inclusion. From a Marxist standpoint the psycho/bio/social model is the successor to the purely social model and the more traditional psycho/bio (special education) model. Via a process of dialectics, the thesis (psycho/bio model) is contested by the social model, which consequently results in a synthesis formed from a fusion of and resolution of both models. Table 7.1 compares the different models according a number of headings or parameters that I hope may highlight differences. I have also chosen phrases from advocates of the different models to represent the key positions. Such an approach is open to bias – which I am happy to acknowledge.

Table 7.1 Comparison of psycho/bio, social and psycho/bio/social models

	Psycho/Bio Model (traditional SEN)	Social Model	Psycho/Bio/Social
Paradigm	Positivist	Modern/ Postmodern	Promiscuous (multiple paradigm) Bricolage? (Lévi-Strauss) Where a range of methodologies are used to represent an area

	Psycho/Bio Model (traditional SEN)	Social Model	Psycho/Bio Model
Aims	Remediation, therapy and care, separate provision	Inclusive society	Enabling the realisation of the long-term goals of education: Active stakeholder Citizenship: possessor of cultural capital
Concepts and premises	Diagnosis and treatment	Diversity is a resource not a barrier	Enablement
		'Indices are about facilitating participation rather than participation *per se*' Ainscow *(1999, p. 150)*	Proximal Zones (Vygotsky, 1986) For all learners and institutions (but not an excuse for 'unreadiness')
		Traditional interventions have failed therefore methods more congruent with the ways mainstream schools work and teachers teach should be employed to improve the quality of education for all	Universal design principles where curricula are designed, planned and implemented to take into account diversity
		Teaching is personalised rather than individualised	
		Constructivist: Knowledge is socially constructed	Constructive Alternativism with different knowledge building tools for different tasks
	Reductionist	Abstraction: the deconstruction of models and decontextualisation via the search for common generic issues and themes across schools in different countries	Contextualisation Developing the professional stock of knowledge (Shultz) within an organisation/system required to enable its learners
		Induction: the generation robust generalities	

	Psycho/Bio Model (traditional SEN)	Social Model	Psycho/Bio/Social
Viewpoint on the individual	Constructed from psychological measures and medical profile	Personalisation rather than individualisation. The teacher makes the topic shared with peers relevant to the learner	Individuals are not always neurotypical, i.e. people may be different. They may think and experience the world differently from their peers due to a variety of factors
Concept of difficulty, disaffection and/or disability	Within child	These concepts are socially constructed so can be deconstructed through language which impacts upon attitudes and practice	Acknowledges social aspects alongside psychological and biological aspects. Some facts cannot be deconstructed but may be reconstructed in alternative ways that may help the learner, her peers, her parents and other professionals
View of diversity	Normative	Diversity is a resource	The whole is more than the sum of its parts. Diversity realistically presents real challenges to education. Therefore, we need to be strategic and politically aware in responding to diversity. We need tools to map diversity and achievement
Stakeholder view point	As client or recipient	Conditional upon agreement on inclusion as defined	Enabled, heard, and fairly represented as part of a developing negotiation of roles and responsibilities in decision-making. Acknowledging consensus and conflicts

	Psycho/Bio Model (traditional SEN)	Social Model	Psycho/Bio/Social
View of technology	Diagnosis, task analysis and programmed learning can improve achievement	Technology is absent from the discourse. Is this because ... Technology is an instrument to further divide the 'information rich' world from the 'countries of the south'?	Technology is changing education and communities. We need to evaluate and guide its use so that it is enabling technology
Methodology	Clinical Reductionism	Reflective practitioner/benign professional Comparative case study Discourse analysis Hermeneutics But not negative case analysis Deconstruction	Case study Negative case analysis Questionnaire Video interview and observation Hermeneutics Action research Single subject Research (IEPs)
Evidence base	Clinical/ professional practice	A small number of schools in economically deprived areas Personal accounts	Qualitative and qualitative data from different levels of analysis
Rigour	Reliability and validity measures	Member checks ? Inter-rater agreement?	Positivist and post positivist measures of reliability and validity as appropriate e.g. Gubba and Lincoln (1998)
Blindspot	The rights of the individual	The individual The future	...?...

7.2 The social model's conception of expertise

Ainscow (1999) is wary of external expertise from outside the school. He states:

> *'Very often much of the expertise that was needed in order to reach out to all learners was already there.'*

'less about importing ideas ... and more to do with finding ways of making better use of local knowledge.'

'Teachers know more than they use ... "the" task of development becomes one of helping teachers and those supporting them to analyse their own practice.'

Is this not an apology for parochialism? It goes against the emerging trend of clusters of schools and services and ignores the online self-help networks that have been demonstrated to have an impact (Wedell, 2000). The impact of the folk psychology of the classroom upon a school's response to diversity has not been explored extensively. It has been suggested by Garner (2001) and Croll and Moses (2000) – and also by researchers in the field of emotional and behavioural difficulty such as Clements and Zarkowska (2000) – that teachers' uncontested theories can lead to the exclusion of some learners from meaningful learning activities. *In extremis* learners can also be excluded from the school. The advent of the Disability Discrimination Act in the United Kingdom, which is now to be applied to schools, may have dramatic results in challenging the ongoing practices within schools based upon the folk psychology of teaching. It is unclear from Ainscow (1999) who 'those supporting them' will be, especially if importing ideas is downplayed.

7.3　What methods of working are valued?

The reflective practitioner model (Schön, 1991) is central to the endeavour of the social model with an endorsement of comparative methods of investigation:

'Where the strange is made familiar and the familiar strange.'

Booth and Ainscow, 1998

'The power of comparison is not from lifting approaches and moving them from place to place .... But from using the stimulus of more exotic environments to reconsider thinking and practice in familiar settings .... Features normally ignored become clearer, possibilities overlooked are reconsidered and things taken for granted are subject to new scrutiny.'

Ainscow, 1999, p. 2

It is presumably preferable to sit under a palm tree in Costa Rica thinking about the implications of schooling in a Third World country for UK schools rather than comparing a non-selective secondary school in North

Canterbury with a selective school in South Canterbury. The emphasis within the purely social model might be tentatively summarised by the following phrase: *'It is not about resources or technologies; it is about the will to be inclusive.'*

The psycho/bio/social model would accept that the willingness to change has to be a starting point but then resources and ways of working will have a lot to do with it. Legislation may also help institutions to find the will. The recent Teacher Training Agency Standards for Special Needs Co-ordinators (SENCos) and specialist teachers (TTA, 1998, 1999) explicitly recognise the importance of knowledge, understanding and skills development in responding to 'severe and complex learning needs', a term whose value is contested within the discourse of the social model.

7.4   The language of individual difference

The purely social model rejects the deficit approach to individuals, which leads to language that denigrates the learner. The use of language can challenge stereotypical entrenched thinking and practice by re-framing issues. However, this new language must enable action rather than the adoption of euphemisms or vagueness. There can be little change when 'the child with special needs' becomes 'the included child'. Ainscow's (1999) phrase regarding 'pupils ... whose progress is a matter of concern', can only lead to the inevitable follow-up question, 'What do you actually mean?' It may be more challenging to state that 'Twenty per cent of the children we teach do not make the same progress as their peers.' rather than 'Twenty per cent of children have special educational needs.'

The social model explicitly fails to respond to individual difference:

> *'the children sometimes referred to as having special needs represent hidden voices that could inform and guide improvement activities in the future. In this sense, as my colleague Susan Hart [1992] has suggested, special needs are special in that they provide insights into possibilities for development that might otherwise pass unnoticed.*

Ainscow, 1999, p. 12

Are 'they' (I think you know who I mean) the curriculum canaries who are not worthy of due consideration in their own right but only if their failures can be utilised for the greater good of the greatest number?

Is it valid to assume that a barrier to learning encountered by a child can always be applicable to the rest of the class or is it that an individual response may in fact be necessary and desirable? For example, a child who has a social communication difficulty may not interpret teaching practices in the same way as their peers. Similarly, a learner with a significant visual impairment may not understand the usage of a Windows-based computer with mouse control. The psycho/bio/social model can harness the principles of Universal Design (CAST, 1998) to enable these learners by creating activities that are in an appropriate modality, with appropriate means of interaction and meaningful feedback.

7.5 Inclusion or fusion: fighting past battles or engineering the future?

The social model ironically has failed to recognise the sociocultural impact of Information Communications Technology (ICT) upon society and especially within education where the most dramatic impact has been with enabling technology (Blamires, 1999). The findings from the authoritative US President's Committee of Advisors on Science and Technology: Panel on Educational Technology (1997) report on the effectiveness of educational technology are telling in relation to under-achievement and special educational needs (SEN). The Committee sees the long-term re-structuring of education within a constructivist learning paradigm where:

> *'Our children will thus need to be prepared not just with a larger set of acts or a larger repertoire of specific skills, but with the capacity to readily acquire new knowledge, to solve new problems and to employ creativity and critical thinking in the design of new approaches to existing problems.'*

1997, p. 9

The report further suggests that traditional models of pedagogy are being changed by the impact of technology in that the following are happening:

◆ Greater attention is given to the acquisition of higher-order thinking and problem-solving skills, with less emphasis on the assimilation of a large body of isolated facts.
◆ Basic skills are learned not in isolation but in the course of undertaking (often on a collaborative basis) higher level 'real-world' tasks whose execution requires the integration of a number of such skills.

◆ Information resources are made available to be accessed by the student at that point in time when they actually become useful in executing the particular task at hand.

◆ Fewer topics may be covered than is the case within the typical traditional curriculum, but these topics are often explored in greater depth.

◆ The student assumes a central role as the active architect of his or her own knowledge and skills, rather than passively absorbing information proffered by the teacher.

The traditional role of the teacher, that is central to the social model's focus on school inclusion, appears to be under pressure of change.

However, the report notes that there are issues of 'equitable access'. Technology does lead to improvements in learning achievement but low achieving students have less in-school access to computers than higher achievers. It emphasises that:

1997 p. 34

> 'While high achievers may be allowed to use computers in the performance of relatively complex "authentic" tasks involving the acquisition and integration of a wide range of factual and procedural knowledge, low achieving students are more likely to be assigned extensive drill and practice on isolated tasks presumably on the assumption that remediation in these areas is a prerequisite to activities requiring higher level thinking and problem solving.'

The social model of school inclusion in the UK has aligned itself to school level target setting to raise standards. The number of secondary schools using Success Maker (a networked largely programmed learning system) is increasing and may represent the trends identified in the American report. Ainscow (1999) quotes Postman in the *New Statesman*, 23 August 1996, in denying the importance of Information Communications Technology:

> 'As you go through and look at our most serious problems, you'll see they have little to do with information. They are not amenable to technological solutions. But a lot of people think that technology is the only way we should go. So there is a real sense that we may be distracted from addressing the real causes of these problems.'

He further comments:

'In many ways the arguments that I have developed ... reflect a similar view. They reject the idea that inclusion is an empirical question that requires us to first of all prove that providing a shared education for all children within a community is effective. They also cast considerable doubt on the assumption that further technological progress is necessary in order to achieve more inclusive forms of schooling.'

It is ironic that while Ainscow embraces the technological rationalism of school improvement, he denies the real impact that ICT already has demonstrated in enabling teachers, parents and learners to participate and find a voice in education.

7.6   Using Foucault's toolbox for analysis

Table 7.2 makes use of categories suggested by Foucault in order to outline further differences between the three models. What appear to be obscure terms are briefly explained in Table 7.2.

Table 7.2 Foucault's toolbox in comparisons of psycho/bio, social and psycho/bio/social models

	Psycho/Bio Model (traditional SEN)	Social Model	Psycho/Bio/Social
Foucault's Tool:			
Surveillance	Upon the child	Upon the school	Variable Upon the learner/ teacher/parent/ administrator/para-professional/ institutions and clusters of institutions
Subject and power	The child subject to control and restraint	Benevolence from professionals working 'in the best interests of all'	Partnership and conflict – negotiating power relationships. Enablement of disadvantaged groups particularly individuals with disability and/or learning difficulty/ disaffection

	Psycho/Bio Model (traditional SEN)	Social Model	Psycho/Bio/Social
Spatialisation	Isolation or segregation	Common occupation of a physical space	Communities are made up of multiple spaces occupied by different groupings with different purposes for a variety of durations. Psycho/bio/social factors can influence membership of these groupings
Archaeology 'A description of discourse – the statements that stand for truth'	'The stigma which was attached to schools for mentally defective children has been partly but not completely shaken off by the later and more enlightened provision for educationally subnormal children.' Tansley and Gulliford (1960) 'The experience of schools confirms that there are many children who are so backward in basic subjects that they need special help.' Tansley and Gulliford (1960)	'special educational needs (SEN) establishes a categorical status signifying deficit and failure in students, directing attention away from problems in teaching and school organisation and constructing a discourse around resources and "needs" rather than student preferences and rights.' Fulcher (1989) 'reach out to the commonality of all students' Ainscow (1999) 'We regard inclusion and exclusion as processes rather than as events and define them respectively as the processes of increasing and reducing the participation of students in the curricula, cultures and communities of neighbourhood mainstream schools' Booth and Ainscow (1998, p. 194)	'Special Educational Needs result from the interaction of social, biological and psychological factors' Norwich (1990)

	Psycho/Bio Model (traditional SEN)	Social Model	Psycho/Bio/Social
		'the privileging of disability issues in the inclusion debate is serving to conceal the extent to which other groups are excluded' Booth and Ainscow (1998)	
Genealogy 'The exercise of power at a micro level'		'Our decision to listen to the views of a randomly selected group of students was part of an overall approach to understanding processes of inclusion and exclusion' Booth and Ainscow (1998)	'Mainstream schools, for their part, will need to become far more effective in assessing the needs of their pupils and must be encouraged to work more closely with special schools in order to identify how teaching approaches, curriculum context and resources which were previously unavailable in mainstream, may be targeted to support those pupils who are currently failing to learn' Rose and Howley (2001)
Ethics 'Ways in which individuals acquire new forms of activity'	'Absences from school, unfortunate personal circumstances, or inadequate environmental conditions have often further limited their progress. Failure to recognise and provide for their problems must be counted among the contributory causes of their backwardness.' Tansley and Gulliford (1960, p. 7) Some children in this group may derive considerable benefit from education in a special school, particularly if their problems require close personal teaching which cannot be provided otherwise	'teachers who do not discriminate against "them" as opposed to "us" but nevertheless, acknowledge and respect differences of impairment, culture and other experiences that shape the individual.' (Booth and Ainscow, 1998) 'These teachers "discriminate" in the sense that they attend to the particular requirements of individual students, but they do this in the context of accepting responsibility for the education of all children in their community.' Ballard (1999, p.169)	'Pedagogical decision-making holds the greatest promise of doing two things – rebutting presumptions that just don't fit, and preventing failures for students who are falling behind. ... we can draw upon the roots of our field to help us further productive partnerships with parents and professional colleagues that utilise research based strategies and target success for exceptional learners.' Crockett (2001)

	Psycho/Bio Model (traditional SEN)	Social Model	Psycho/Bio/Social
			The 'move towards an apprenticeship model (of teacher training) involving on the job training ... results in less time for the consideration of important conceptual issues' Garner (2001)
			'Enablement is about being helped to achieve something that could not be achieved at all without aid or without great personal effort. An individual may be enabled to learn something, say something, do something, create something, go somewhere or join in some activity. Enabling technology is not just about access, it is about engagement and inclusion'. Blamires, (1999, p. 1)

7.7   Discussion

The tools show surprising similarities. The traditional and social models appear to share benevolence in their response to diversity with their truth statements. It was difficult to locate statements within the psycho/bio/social area as many researchers and practitioners have not explicitly located their work within this model as yet. The comparison indicates reluctance within the social model of school inclusion to tolerate networking and outside interference within the project. It has been claimed within the social model that individuals with difficulty or disability were marginalised within the traditional model, however, the extreme social model exhibits a benevolent paternalism that further segregates individuals who are denied the language of physical, cognitive or emotional difference. Allan (1999) has noted what can happen when a dominant social model is challenged, for example, by blind students whose obvious difference was not referred to: a little bit like *Fawlty Towers*, where you must at all costs, 'not mention the war'.

7.8   Conclusion

This chapter has pinpointed limitations of the social model that has succeeded the traditional special education model of difficulty, diversity and disaffection. The psycho/bio/social model builds on the strengths of previous models that may result in a radical fusion. The use of Foucault's toolbox highlights underlying issues dealing with the application of power and engagement in decision-making across the three models and attempts to make them explicit for users and consumers of this model. The social model is necessary as a tool to support inclusion but, by itself, it is not sufficient to provide frameworks and guidance necessary for the implementation and evaluation of inclusive practice.

References

Ainscow, M. *Understanding the Development of Inclusive Schools*, London, Falmer Press, 1999.

Allan, J. *Actively Seeking Inclusion: Pupils with Special Needs in Mainstream Schools*, London, Falmer Press, 1999.

Armstrong, F., Armstrong, D. and Barton, L. (eds) *Inclusive Education: Policy, Contexts and Comparative Perspectives*, London, David Fulton Publishers, 1999. ·

Ballard, K. (ed.) *Inclusive Education: International Voices on Disability and Justice*, London, Falmer Press, 1999.

Blamires, M. (ed.) *Enabling Technology for Inclusion*, London, Sage and Paul Chapman, 1999.

Booth, T. and Ainscow, M. (eds) *From Them to Us: An International Study of Inclusion and Education*, London, Routledge, 1998.

Clark, C., Dyson, A. and Millward, A. (eds) *Theorising Special Education*, London, Routledge, 1998.

Clements, J. and Zarkowska, E. *Approaches to Challenging Behaviour in Autism*, London, Jessica Kingsley Publishers, 2000.

Corbett, J. *Bad-Mouthing: The Language of Special Needs*, London, Falmer Press, 1996.

Crockett, J.B. 'Beyond inclusion: preventing disabilities from handicapping the futures of our children', Chapter 6 in this volume, 2001.

Croll, P. and Moses, D. *One in Five: The Assessment and Incidence of Special Educational Needs*, London, Routledge and Kegan Paul, 1985.

Croll, P. and Moses, D. 'Ideologies and utopias: educational professionals' view of inclusion', *European Journal of Special Needs Education* 15 (1), 2000, pp. 1–12.

Fulcher, G. *Disabling Policies: A Comparative Approach to Education Policy and Disability*, London, Falmer Press, 1989.

Garner, P. 'Goodbye Mr Chips', Chapter 4 in this volume, 2001.

Hall, J. *Social Devaluation and Special Education: The Right to Full Mainstream Inclusion and an Honest Statement*, London, Jessica Kingsley, 1998.

Hornby, G. 'Promoting responsible inclusion: quality education for all', Chapter 1 in this volume, 2001.

Norwich, B. *Reappraising Special Needs Education*, London, Cassell, 1990.

President's Committee of Advisors on Science and Technology: Panel on Educational Technology, *Report to the President on the Use of Technology to Strengthen K-12 Education in the United States*, 1997, www.whitehouse.gov/wh/EOP/OSTP/NSTC/PCAST/k-12ed.html

Rose, R. and Howley, M. 'Entitlement or denial?: the curriculum and its influences upon inclusion processes, Chapter 5 in this volume, 2001.

Schön, D. *The Reflective Practitioner: How Professionals Think in Action*, Aldershot: Ashgate-Arena, 1991.

Tansley, A.E. and Gulliford, R. *The Education of the Slow Learning Child*, London, Routledge, 1960.

Teacher Training Agency *National Special Educational Needs Specialist Standards*, London, TTA, 1999.

Teacher Training Agency *National Standards for Special Educational Needs Co-ordinators,* London, TTA, 1998.

Thomas, G., Webb, J. and Walker, D. *The Making of the Inclusive School*, London, Routledge, 1997.

Vygotsky, L.S. *Thought and Language*, Cambridge, MA, MIT Press, 1986.

Wedell, K. 'Points from the SENCo-Forum: putting inclusion into practice', *British Journal of Special Education* 27 (2), 2000, p. 100.

Christopher Robertson

8.1 Introduction

This chapter offers some personal, though certainly not comprehensive reflections, on the *social modelling* of inclusive education. It is also worth noting that these are presented from the perspective of someone who is wholeheartedly committed (Robertson, 1998, 2000) to the development of inclusive education and participation across all domains of cultural, social and economic life.

The following words seem to me, to provide a helpful metaphor for how inclusive education is developing in the United Kingdom currently:

> *'We have got on to slippery ice where there is no friction and so in a certain sense the conditions are ideal, but also, just because of that, we are unable to walk. We want to walk: so we need* friction. *Back to the rough ground!'*

Wittgenstein, 1997

Put differently, and certainly less eloquently, is the current drive towards inclusive educational practice taking place on 'very thin ice'? Is a central plank, or foundation of claims made for inclusive practice – *the social model* (Booth *et al.*, 2000) – going to be able to support the education of *all* learners in mainstream schools? Or is it the case that *'one might teach by this model on ice but hardly in the rough ground of the classroom'*. (Dunne, 1993, p. 5)

The rest of this chapter considers how robust some aspects of the social model of disability are in their application to education. Some elements of parallel discussion may be noted in the preceding chapter by Mike Blamires. However, my specific concern is with the use of a social model of disability developed originally by disabled academics and activists (Oliver, 1996, p. 30) in educational contexts.

8.2 Thin ice

I want to suggest that the social modelling of inclusion (Oliver, 1992, 1996) is both reductionist, and in some ways, very unhelpful to education professionals and to the children and young people they teach. In particular, the uncritical use of such modelling to shape or mould purportedly inclusive policies is likely, in the long term, to be counter-productive and lead to separatist practices as its naïvety is exposed. This modelling of inclusion is often summarised as shown in Figure 8.1.

Figure 8.1 Disability models

Integration	or	Inclusion
State	or	Process
Non-problematic	or	Problematic
Professional and administrative approaches	or	Politics
Changes in school organisation	or	Changes in school ethos
Teachers acquire skills	or	Teachers acquire commitment
Curriculum delivery must change	or	Curriculum content must change
Legal rights to integration	or	Moral and political rights to inclusion
Acceptance and tolerance of children with SEN	or	Valuation and celebration of children with SEN
Normality	or	Difference
Integration can be delivered	or	Inclusion must be struggled for

Source: Adapted from Oliver (1996). Note: I have used the word 'or' in the table to indicate that the models are often used in absolute ways, in terms of bad or good.

This modelling of education is derived from wider concerns about the experience of disability (Finkelstein, 1980; Oliver 1983) and the generation of a model to analyse this. Modelling of this type, and here it is important to emphasise the pioneering value of this, has informed much disability awareness training and disability-equality training in educational contexts (e.g. Rieser and Mason, 1992, and the work of the Disability Equality in Education organisation).

There are, however, significant problems with this modelling, and its application to education. These include the following:

◆ A tendency to discuss complexity in simple terms, or polarities that do not reflect reality (Engel, 1977; Norwich, 1994).

◆ Unclear conceptualisations of disability, with a tendency to ignore the interests of children and young people with significant learning difficulties or emotional and behavioural difficulties (EBD).

◆ Dismissal of the history of special education as essentially segregationist and damaging. Cole (1989) and Hurt (1988) have countered simplistic misreadings of history, and Armstrong (1998) has identified complex strands in moves towards inclusive educational practice that can be traced back over a century.

◆ The propagation of outdated perspectives on the strengths and weaknesses of special schools. A review report on education in special schools and units undertaken by the Office for Standards in Education (OfSTED, 1999) covering the period 1994 to 1998 notes significant improvements, particularly in 1997/8 *when standards rose more quickly, so that pupils made at least satisfactory progress in nine out of ten schools. This is a proportion comparable with mainstream schools'*. This view of special schools challenges the notion that pupils attending special schools receive an inferior education, at least in terms of academic standards. 1999, p. 11

◆ The use of blunt instrument critiques of psychological perspectives. These tend to operate through the use of crude distinctions and assumptions, e.g. the individual model = psychology = bad (with medical and pathological associations), the social model = sociology = good (with emancipatory associations).

◆ A hierarchical view of knowledge, as opposed to a pluralist one (Engel, 1980; Cooper, 1996) is advocated, with a quasi-sociological epistemology portrayed as most truthful.

◆ A commitment to one particular educational value (e.g. equality) and a consequent tendency to disregard other important values (Berlin, 1998; Lunt and Norwich, 1999) that clash with it.

◆ The lack of reference to key aspects of educational policy such as standards of achievement, and parental choice (Howe, 1997). These central features of educational policy present major tensions for both the theory and practice of inclusive education.

Each of these 'problems' could be discussed in more detail, and the references cited simply 'signpost' relevant literature that indicate difficulties that the social modelling of inclusive education has failed to take account of as yet. There are many things I would want to defend in the kind of inclusive education model outlined in Figure 8.1. However, the problems of such a model, particularly when *applied* through professional development in schools (see Booth *et al.*, 2000, p. 108) and other educational settings, need to be recognised if moves towards inclusion are not founded on reductionism and misrepresentation of a kind that will alienate teachers. To illustrate why the use of a social model presents such difficulties I will look more closely at four of the ten dimensions listed in Figure 8.1 that most directly refer to education.

8.2.1 Inclusion as a process (as opposed to a state)

This claim for inclusion is, at one level, a statement of the obvious. However, little is said from a social perspective about issues of pedagogy that lie at the heart of this process. With this in mind, it is worth noting that Lindsay (1997) and Lindsay and Thompson (1997), writing from what might be construed as a more psychological approach, have highlighted some politically pragmatic ways forward in the planning and study of inclusion. This realism is of the kind harnessed to innovation and political leadership that has informed the development of interesting inclusive practice in Spain (Pastor, 1998; Marchesi, 1993). Close, and theoretically rigorous, knowledge of this kind of international development would be more useful to educators than descriptive comparative accounts of inclusive educational policies (Artiles and Larsen, 1998).

The social model of inclusion, if it is to move beyond critique, needs to present a more rigorous and pragmatic view of the educational process. To do this, I suggest that some *rough* ideological ground has to be walked upon, and connections with academics from different disciplines, teachers, students and parents have to be made. Unless this ground is covered, the process view of inclusion is likely to remain at fairly abstract level. Promisingly, work by Allan (1999) and Corbett (2000) does explore the process of inclusion in a connected way, and shows how it is both possible and necessary to move beyond models to bring about positive change within schools that operate under significant constraints.

8.2.2 Schools need to change their ethos (rather than organisation)

Advocating changes in educational ethos to make schools more welcoming communities for all learners is essential, but this can only be achieved in a limited way unless wider policies of education move beyond a rhetoric of inclusion. Schools alone, though they may strive heroically to develop inclusive practices, are currently continually bombarded with conflicting demands, most of which call upon them to work exclusively. If such exclusivity is to be challenged, then the social model of inclusion needs to aim its critique much more clearly at the educational policy that emerges from the Department for Education and Employment (DfEE). The power of exclusive educational policies remains predominant, and it is this that needs combating, for, as Howe (1997), commenting on education in the USA notes:

> '*Equality of educational opportunity is under siege. It has been identified both as the chief culprit in "dumbing down" the curriculum and as the tool of arrogant, know-it-all bureaucrats. So long as the average classroom remains the kind of dismal, mind-numbing place it is; so long as performing well in the traditional high track curriculum provides the ticket to expanded opportunity; and so long as inadequate funding forces difficult choices, pressures will persist to stratify the public schools in order to ensure that the most talented receive a good education. Given currently prevailing political winds, responding to promote the welfare of these children threatens to come at the expense of less advantaged ones.*'

1997, p. 90

Commenting on educational policy in the UK, Slee (1998) draws a similar conclusion and suggests that '*Inclusive education is dismissive of the assimilationist imperative of school effectiveness and the National Curriculum.*' However, I would suggest that the social model of disability, in so far as it has impacted on education in the UK, has remained too silent on how to change the ethos of government policy. As such, it has actually been used in an assimilationist mode, of the kind Slee rejects. At the current time, 'tools' or 'manuals' for working towards inclusive practice – such as the *Index for Inclusion* (Booth *et al.*, 2000) and *Success for Everyone in Schools: Standards for Inclusive Educational Practice in Schools* (Bonathon *et al.*, 2000) – may all too easily be used in mechanical ways that do not address fundamental issues of change necessary to achieve their stated aims.

As well as addressing the politic of school ethos more directly, more positive connections need to be made between perspectives based on a social model of inclusion and important work on curriculum theory and pedagogy (Edwards and Kelly, 1998; Noddings, 1992). Only when such connections are made, can changes in school ethos be fully realised.

8.2.3 Teachers require commitment (rather than skills)

This claim of the social model of inclusion is rather a frightening one. Without engaging in a well-worn discussion about general and specialist teaching, it is worth noting that, for many years now, teachers entering the profession have expressed grave concern about their lack of skills in the area currently described as special education (Garner, 2001; Robertson, 1999). Quite simply, whether we are talking about newly qualified teachers (NQTs) or more experienced teachers, the lack of concern or respect for *their* views, implicit in the social model of inclusion, on what is needed to prepare them to teach across pupil diversity is profoundly discouraging. When the educational needs of children are couched in terms of rights, it surely seems appropriate that teachers should have the right to be prepared to teach a wide range of learners effectively.

The recent introduction of *National Special Educational Needs Specialist Standards* (TTA, 1999) has been seen by at least one commentator (Booth, 2000), as part of the perpetuation of an exclusionary approach to teacher education. Such a stance seems to me to be simplistic and damaging, both to the teaching profession and to children and young people experiencing difficulties in learning. It is simplistic in the way that it ignores different perspectives on the need for specialisation, e.g. those of other education professionals, non-government organisations, and parental lobby groups. The introduction of the aforementioned specialist standards for example, was delayed as much by objections from groups wanting more detail as well as those claiming they were exclusionary (Booth, 2000, p. 90). It is damaging in the way that it implies that a deskilled educational workforce working in an at best, an ambivalent policy context, will be able to develop inclusive educational practice. This refusal to walk the rough ground seems to point to a future educational outcome where special schools will re-emerge as 'best practice', and where parents choose these for their children because of the 'specialist expertise' unavailable in mainstream provision. It may be that this is already happening. A glance at job advertisements in the educational press indicates that in various parts of the UK plans are in place to open new special schools for pupils with EBD, for pupils with complex learning needs, and that schools are re-branding their expertise.

I would suggest that the social model of inclusion has failed to recognise that specialist teacher knowledge, skills and understanding are an essential part of achieving more inclusive educational provision. It is also not conceptually incoherent to talk of inclusion and specialisation together. Withers (1986) was right in arguing that teachers working in the field of special education need to develop greater sympathy (as opposed to empathy) *with* their pupils and to express their commitment and solidarity to the achievement of full educational participation. This sympathy, though, must be harnessed to more appropriate teacher specialisation opportunities that build on initial teacher education practice of the kind advocated by Garner in this volume. Radical rethinking is required to address generic and specialist training for both teachers and learning support assistants, otherwise inclusive educational practice will remain the educational remit of only some teachers as Sarason (1990) has noted:

> '*School personnel are graduates of our colleges and universities. It is there that they learn that there are at least two types of human beings, and if you choose to work with one of them you render yourself legally and conceptually incompetent to work with others.*'

1990, p. 258

Attempts to address this dilemma for inclusive education are emerging in the USA, where Ferguson (2000) for example, has suggested new *hybrid* teachers are needed to ensure that inclusive educational practice takes root. She has also argued that new approaches to *group practice* in teaching are required, whereby groups of teachers with a range of skills are collectively responsible for groups of diverse learners. These ways forward show great promise, but they require that a *commitment alone* position on pedagogy be abandoned.

8.2.4 Curriculum content rather than delivery must change

The model of disability referred to in this chapter has little to say about the complexities of curriculum theory and practice. Instead, it focuses on the inadequacies of *segregated* schooling where '*curriculum delivery is inadequate in most special schools*' (Oliver, 1996). I am not offering a defence of such practice, but suggest that a simplistic view of more recent developments is conveyed by advocates of a social model of inclusion who draw solely on disability politics. Without wishing to be seen as a supporter of the OfSTED approach to school inspection, it is interesting to note in the 1994–98 review of special education in specialist settings mentioned earlier in this chapter, significant and positive developments were made in curriculum provision. This might suggest that one of the key tenets of educational inclusion advocated by the social model is conceptualised in a rather outdated way. Of course, this does not mean that complacency is acceptable, nor does it mean that current specialist 'status quo' provision should remain. It does mean, however, that inaccurate views of practice cannot be the drivers of change.

This brings me to the central point made by advocates of the social model of inclusion, namely, that the curriculum is disablist (see Rieser and Mason, 1992). I would agree that some curriculum materials used in schools have been disablist – for example, children's literature – and this issue still needs to be addressed. What we need here are developments concerned with changing aspects of curriculum content (DfEE, 1999a). I would like to see, for example, poetry by disabled writers (e.g. Lois Keith's excellent *Mustn't Grumble,* 1994) included in the English syllabus. I would also like to see important issues of bioethics introduced to the curriculum in secondary schools so that the possibility of new eugenics and disability can be critically appraised (Guyer, 2000) by young people. At the same time, the curriculum as a whole needs to be challenged in more radical ways of the kind I have referred to earlier when discussing issues of school ethos. The social model of inclusion has, to date, focused too singularly on disability issues, and neglected the implications of these for curriculum theory.

I am not convinced either, that 'problems' of disability and the curriculum can be solved by disability awareness staff development activity in schools, of the kind delivered by organisations such as Disability Equality in Education Training alone. This approach, delivered by disabled trainers, and which I think is extremely important, makes significant use of social models of both disability of and inclusion. It also, however, makes particular claims of the kind referred to already in this chapter and presents a partial and not always coherent view of inclusive educational developments. For example, an information leaflet published by the organisation states that:

> *'Inclusion also paves the way for school improvement and effectiveness. In schools where all pupils are included and where the teaching and learning have been developed to meet specific needs, achievement for all pupils has been seen to improve faster than in schools with a non-inclusive ethos.'*

Disability Equality in
Education, 1999

Space precludes a detailed unravelling of the intended meaning of this quotation, but it clearly contains contentious and contradictory statements. Just one example of this can be seen in the reference to *'teaching and learning developed ... to meet specific needs'*. This comment would seem to imply that pupils with specific needs should have these addressed in specific (special?) ways. Yet, the social model of inclusion does not seem to hold a place for specialist teaching skills. Disability awareness and equality training for schools need to take more account of educational diversity and complexity. In this way it can build on its important achievements to date, and in doing this it also needs to recognise different voices within the disabled community (e.g. Low, 1997; Morris, 1991) and those of many other disenfranchised learners bearing the special educational needs label.

To summarise, the social model of inclusion needs to provide a more rigorous and robust account of the kind of curriculum change necessary to meet the needs of all learners. Until it does this, we need to be cautious about the value of its analysis of special and mainstream education. We also need to be supportive but critical of disability equality training in educational settings. It may be that such training will have a significant part to play in the education of children and young people and inform the teaching of Citizenship in particular (DfEE, 1999b) within the National Curriculum 2000. But such training will need to overcome a tendency to *explain away* tensions and dilemmas in inclusive education if it is to contribute to changing practice of the kind it is committed to achieving.

8.3   Terra firma

My criticisms of dimensions and aspects of the social model of inclusion have been made from the standpoint of someone who has strong sympathies (Withers, 1986) with achieving greater equity in education, and wider social justice within a rich social theory of disability (Oliver, 1991). However, a theoretical account of inclusion, which I suggest must be hermeneutic in kind, has to develop on the rough ground where values are discussed, disputed, and referenced to empirical understanding. A social model of inclusion has much to contribute to both the theory and practice of inclusion, but it currently provides a flawed explanatory framework for bringing about change within education complexity and contradiction.

For the foreseeable future compromise solutions to the *problem* of inclusive education are likely to be the norm. Explanations of old practice (integration and segregation) and guidance on how the new (inclusion) can be forged need to recognise that:

> '*two factors are likely to determine the outcomes of the present debate. The first is the commitment of parents of students with disabilities to a quality education and the second is the goal of the state to confine*

Cole, 1999, p. 225 *the costs of educational and social services within particular budget parameters.'*

In view of such overarching constraints, advocates of the social model of inclusion should collaborate with others to review strengths and weaknesses in both the theory and practice of education for all. This may require a new reciprocity. Humility needs to be established between groups who are habituated in the culture of critique. Tannen (1998), who writes luminously about aggressive positioning within educational debate points to a helpful way forward:

> *'We need to use our imaginations and ingenuity to find different ways to seek truth and gain knowledge, and add them to our arsenal – or should I say, to the ingredients of our stew. It will take creativity to find ways to blunt the most dangerous blades of the argument culture.'*

1998, p. 298

If we heed this advice and move from adversarial debate to dialogue, then inclusive educational policies and practices are much more likely to emerge, than if we continue to oversimplify and to confuse belief as thinking (ibid., p. 280). In other words, we need to walk softly, but on rough ground.

Acknowledgement

I am grateful to Joseph Dunne (1993) through whose writing I first stumbled upon the quotation by Ludwig Wittgenstein used in this chapter.

References

Allan, J. *Actively Seeking Inclusion: Pupils with Special Needs in Mainstream Schools*, London, Falmer Press, 1999.

Armstrong, D. 'Changing places; policy routes to inclusion', in *Managing Inclusive Education: From Policy to Experience*, P. Clough. (ed.), London, Paul Chapman, 1998.

Artiles, A. and Larsen, L. 'Learning from special education reform movements in four continents', *European Journal of Special Needs Education* 13 (1), 1998, pp. 5–9.

Berlin, I. *The Proper Study of Mankind: An Anthology of Essays*, edited by Henry Hardy and Roger Hausheer, London, Pimlico, 1998.

Bonathon, M., Edwards, G. and Leadbetter, J. *Success for Everyone in Schools: Standards for Inclusive Educational Practice*, Birmingham, Birmingham Advisory and Support Service, 2000.

Booth, T. 'Inclusion and exclusion policy in England: who controls the agenda?', in *Inclusive Education: Policy, Contexts and Comparative Perspectives*, F. Armstrong, D. Armstrong and L. Barton, (eds), London, David Fulton, 2000.

Booth, T., Ainscow, M., Black-Hawkins, K., Vaughan, M. and Shaw, L. *Index for Inclusion: Developing Learning and Participation in Schools*, Bristol, Centre for Studies on Inclusive Education (CSIE), 2000.

Cole, P. 'The structure and arguments used to support or oppose inclusion policies for students with disabilities', *Journal of Intellectual and Developmental Disability* 24 (3), 1999, pp. 215–25.

Cole, T. *Apart or A Part? Integration and the Growth of Special Education*, Milton Keynes, Open University Press, 1989.

Cooper, P. 'Giving it a name: the value of descriptive categories in educational approaches to emotional and behavioural difficulties', *Support for Learning* 11 (4), 1996, pp. 146–50.

Corbett, J. '*Approaching a pedagogy which supports inclusive education*', paper presented as part of a symposium on the politics of pedagogy at the International Special Education Congress 2000, University of Manchester, 24–28 July 2000.

Department for Education and Employment *From Exclusion to Inclusion: A Report of the Disability Rights Task Force on Civil Rights for Disabled People*, London, DfEE (http://www.disability.gov.uk), 1999a.

Department for Education and Employment *Citizenship: The National Curriculum for England*, published jointly with the Qualifications and Curriculum Authority, London, HMSO, 1999b, www.nc.uk.net

Disability Equality in Education *Are You Prepared for the Future?*, publicity information leaflet, London: Disability Equality, 1999.

Dunne, J. *Back to the Rough Ground: 'Phronesis' and 'Techne' in Modern Philosophy and in Aristotle*, Notre Dame, University of Notre Dame Press, 1993.

Edwards, G. and Kelly, A. *Experience and Education: Towards an Alternative National Curriculum*, London, Paul Chapman, 1998.

Engel, G. 'The need for a new medical model: a challenge for bio-medicine', *Science* 196 (4286), 1977, pp. 129–36.

Engel. G. 'The clinical application of the biopsychosocial model', *The American Journal of Psychiatry* 137 (5), 1980, pp. 535–44.

Ferguson, D. 'Preparing teachers for the future', *The OnPoint Series*, Oregon: National Institute for School Improvement, University of Oregon, 2000. http://www.edc.org/urban

Finkelstein, V. *Attitudes and Disabled People: Issues for Discussion*, New York, World Rehabilitation Fund, 1980.

Garner, P. 'Goodbye Mr Chips', Chapter 4 in this volume, 2001.

Guyer, R. 'The teaching of bioethics in high schools', *Newsletter of the Network of Bioethics and Intellectual Disability* 5 (1), 2000, pp. 1–5.

Howe, K. *Understanding Educational Opportunity: Social Justice, Democracy and Schooling*, New York, Teachers College Press, 1997.

Hurt, J. *Outside the Mainstream*, London, Batsford, 1988.

Keith, L. (ed.) *Mustn't Grumble*, London, The Women's Press, 1994.

Lindsay, G. 'Values, rights and dilemmas', *British Journal of Special Education* 24 (2), 1997, pp. 55–9.

Lindsay, G. and Thompson, D. *Values into Practice in Special Education*, London, David Fulton, 1997.

Low, C. 'Is inclusivism possible?', *European Journal of Special Educational Needs Education* 12 (1), 1997, pp. 71–9.

Lunt, I. and Norwich, B. *Can Effective Schools Be Inclusive Schools?* Perspectives on Education Series, London, Institute of Education, 1999.

Marchesi, A. 'Spanish steps', interview with Stanley Segal, *Special Children* June/July, 1993, pp. 25–6.

Morris, J. *Pride Against Prejudice*, London, Women's Press, 1991.

Noddings, N. *The Challenge of Care: An Alternative to Care in Schools*, New York, Teachers College Press, 1992.

Norwich, B. 'Differentiation: from the perspective of resolving tensions between basic social values and assumptions about individual differences', *Curriculum Studies* 2 (3), 1994, pp. 289–308.

Office for Standards in Education *Special Education 1994–1998: A Review of Special Schools, Secure Units and Pupil Referral Units in England*, London, HMSO, 1999.

Oliver, M. *Social Work with Disabled People*, Basingstoke, Macmillan, 1983.

Oliver, M. *The Politics of Disablement*, Basingstoke, Macmillan, 1991.

Oliver, M. 'Intellectual masturbation: a rejoinder to Soder and Booth', *European Journal of Special Needs Education* 7 (1), 1992, pp. 21–8.

Oliver, M. *Understanding Disability*, Basingstoke, Macmillan, 1996.

Pastor, C.G. 'Integration in Spain: a critical view', *European Journal of Special Needs Education* 13 (1), 1998, pp. 43–56.

Rieser, R. and Mason, M. *Disability Equality in the Classroom: A Human Rights Issue,* London, Disability Equality in Education, 1992.

Robertson, C. 'Quality of life as a consideration in the development of inclusive education for pupils and students with learning difficulties', in *Promoting Inclusive Practice*, C. Tilstone, L. Florian, and R. Rose. (eds), London, Routledge, 1998.

Robertson, C. 'Initial teacher education and inclusive schooling', *Support for Learning* 14 (4), 1999, pp. 169–73.

Robertson, C. (forthcoming) 'Quality of life and the development of inclusive education for children and young people with learning disabilities', in *Psicología educativa: programas y desafíos en educación básica* A. Morales, (ed.) (Colección Archivos; no. 8): Memoria del VI. Mexico: Universidad Pedagogica Nacional.

Sarason, S. *The Predictable Failure of School Reform*, San Francisco, Jossey-Bass, 1990.

Slee, R. 'High reliability organizations and liability students', in *School Effectiveness for Whom? Challenges to the School Effectiveness and School Improvement Movements*, R. Slee, G. Weiner and S. Tomlinson (eds), London, Falmer Press, 1998.

Tannen, D. *The Argument Culture: Changing the Way We Argue*, London, Virago Press, 1998.

Teacher Training Agency *National Special Educational Needs Specialist Standards*, London, TTA, 1999.

Withers, R. 'Having sympathies in special education: an argument for the refusal of empathy', *Disability, Handicap and Society* 1 (2), 1986, pp. 197–205.

Wittgenstein, L. *Philosophical Investigations*, Oxford, Blackwell Publishers, 1997.

Chapter 9

Enabling inclusion: Is the culture of change being responsibly managed?

John Cornwall

9.1   Introduction

The process of developing what is currently termed an inclusive education provision in this country heralds a major organisational and cultural change following many previous and prescribed changes (e.g. DfEE, 1997, 1998; 1998; OfSTED, 1999b). The pace of such continuous educational change in England and Wales, for good or ill, is predominantly politically driven. These changes have been largely reactionary, rather than radical or visionary and sometimes they have been confused and contradictory. Inclusion implies more profound transformations, requiring fundamental shifts of culture and attitude (Dyson, 1997; Booth *et al.*, 1998). The way to 'how' this could be achieved is being given in expert guidance and texts such as exemplified in the *Index for Inclusion* (Booth *et al.*, 2000). Organisational change involves transformation at both group and individual level in order to cope with the subsequent demands emanating from new procedures and expectations. Ultimately, an organisation will not adapt itself successfully to a new situation unless it can influence the behaviour of its members, encourage them to change and adopt new perceptions. All change situations involve people learning to behave in new, and hopefully more effective, ways. They may also have to think and feel in different ways too, possibly about their jobs, their organisation and their working relationships. People are most likely to learn and change when they believe that new behaviour is both desirable and possible, that the new thinking makes sense and that they will achieve some lasting benefits from present tribulation. If inclusion is to be enabled at all, attention needs to be paid to the current process of change and to the conditions that exist that will facilitate or hinder it.

Change itself is usually controversial, often resisted and, in this case, idealistic. Its fundamental principles and philosophy are being scrutinised. Arguments range from the epistemological, in questioning how we know inclusion can work, to ontological (Smith, 1998) discussion about whether inclusion can really exist at all. This chapter contributes questions about the process of change being implemented under the banner of inclusion. It is concerned with the human face of education and the consequences for children, young people and for the adults who care and educate them. Individuals do not necessarily need to change their 'attitudes' for change to be implemented as their behaviour can be changed in the short term (Honey, 1997). The way successive changes have taken place in education over the past ten or more years could be characterised by Peter Honey's (1997) 'force and support' model. While the 'force' element is much in evidence in education through the legislation and expectations mentioned above, the 'support' element is harder to find: *Effective learning requires an atmosphere that offers the kind of relationship and support that compensates for the distressing and disruptive aspects of change'.*

Goldstein, 1984
cited in Furey,
1998

Unless support and encouragement follow swiftly, then changes can come unstuck, 'peter out' or become perverted versions of the original ideal. Lack of consideration for those charged with enacting policy for children and young people (i.e. teachers) is evidenced by politicians 'competing with each other', over the years, to be tough on education (Tomlinson, 2000). It is also implicit in this chapter that the quality of education and enablement that we expect, is dependent upon the morale and commitment of those who teach, form relationships with, and transmit knowledge and culture to children and young people. Inclusion is a state of mind and a process, not a physical location or an outcome.

9.2   The myth of 'excellence' and 'standards'

Planning approaches based on bureaucratic notions about organisational functions often ignore the most important resource, the people involved. This is not to say that governments and politicians shouldn't put forward a broad 'vision' for the education system. Or, that subsequent confusion in implementation is necessarily a direct result of political agendas. However, the overall effect of recent successive waves of legislation has had the effect of de-professionalising and demoralising teachers rather than enabling them. It has ignored the inherent difficulties of meeting diverse individual needs in a competitive and elitist context (Lunt, 1998). For two decades there has been an over-abundance of interventions changing and interfering in the details of school management and class teaching. There is an assumption that 'inclusion' is fully justified by being 'morally right' on the one hand and a government requirement on the other. If it is morally right, then it has always been morally right but has not generated equal interest in the past. Change and growth are never without challenges, struggles and hard work but there comes a point when constant change, conflicting priorities and insecure leadership will wear down the hardiest of troops. The practical consequences of the change process generated by current definitions of 'inclusive practices' should be explored. Dyson (1997, p. 153) gives a perspective on failed intentions in the past two decades: *'The focus of attention came to be on rearranging the ways in which special education was delivered, rather than constructing a form of education which would be equitable in itself and which would promote wider social equity.'* He questions whether successive initiatives have really addressed the inequalities of opportunity and achievement within schools. It is tempting to see the current government stance on inclusion, as a 'Johnny come lately' muscling in to what has been growing ecologically over the past twenty or more years.

Inclusive schools cannot really exist in a milieu of heavy competition and exclusivity. This competitive ethos is still used to denigrate teachers and schools and to remove those said to be 'failing'. This is not a socially responsible policy and nor does it foster confidence towards inclusion. Some schools will not accept pupils because of low attainment or disability. Others because the pupils have not been identified as having a specific type of disability or because their parents do not follow a particular religious philosophy. Parental choice often leads to alternative provision in a system where there is little incentive to work with troubled pupils or those who cannot perform. League tables and politically constructed social stigma provide a significant disincentive for schools to be inclusive. The current short-term 'target-based economy' linked to the political rhetoric of 'standards raising' and a hierarchical view of educational change (top down) militates against successful cultural change.

> *'Organisational response to diversity ... how students are categorised, grouped, taught, supported and disciplined ... provides a framework against which students are valued and inclusion can be understood. An organisation is a culture ... an inclusive school is an elusive ideal, existing when no difference is devalued within society.'*
>
> Booth *et al.*, 1998

If the inclusive alternative currently being proposed is a large, community-based institution in one location, without parental choice and not without competition or selection, it will restrict the notion of 'inclusion' to larger and larger educational factories. In many instances this adherence to a locational view of inclusion makes it nothing more than a rearrangement of pupils into different buildings without significant systemic or cultural change:

Brown, 1997

'Important educational objectives which, for example, focus on helping students from different ethnic and social backgrounds to retain and value their own culture may be at risk if their school experience is construed essentially as one of a simple-minded equality passport into mainstream – a sacrifice to cultural assimilation.'

9.3   Building commitment to change

If cultural changes are to be given the best chance to develop, they need to satisfy many criteria. The criteria for inclusion currently being proffered are often at odds with the prevailing edification of competition and the veneration of traditional academic success. There are no discrete or elegant psychological or conceptual models that can describe the relationship between the individual and the organisation (or society) in terms of change (Walsh, 1996; Bevington, 1999). Nor can we fully explain the consequences (emotional, cognitive or behavioural) for the promotion of joint action in social communities. The possible exception is Kelly's (1955) Personal Construct Psychology (Stam, 1998; Gergen, 1999). However, Kanter (1984) and in her subsequent writing (e.g. Kanter, 1988) is very clear that unless commitment to change is actively sought and built on, the subsequent results will be short-lived and of minimal benefit. These barriers to 'commitment to change' are summarised in Figure 9.1. There is a possibility that 'top-down' changes are likely to be superseded by the next political flavour of the month, well before they have had time to establish themselves. The following paragraphs reflect on key factors that could reduce commitment to such changes.

Loss of control	Excess uncertainty
Unexpected surprises	Unnecessary loss of routine
Loss of face	Competence concerns
Ripple effects	More work
Past resentments	Real threat

Figure 9.1 Summarising Kanter's barriers to commitment to change

Kanter, 1988

'It is not power that corrupts but powerlessness....'

The first barrier to successful and lasting organisational change is *loss of control* by those who are expected to implement and maintain the direct consequence of the changes. There needs to be room for employees, staff or members of any team to participate in decisions and planning (short and long term). The terms 'special' and 'special education' have also become impugned and yet, in practice, they are characterised by a greater emphasis upon empowerment through the following:

◆ more actual contact between teacher and pupil;
◆ more focused and detailed teaching methods;
◆ the use of specialist approaches;
◆ additional specialist resources;
◆ learning support (usually multi-professional), and;
◆ a learning environment that encourages confidence, motivation and activation.

There is a danger that, because teachers have lost control of their professional arena, these positive attributes will also be lost. Both special and mainstream educators have spent much time and effort over the past thirteen years trying to create meaningful educational experiences for students with additional needs, within the confinement of a *'rigid and inappropriate hierarchy of knowledge'* (Dyson, 1997).

Excess uncertainty can be reduced by involvement in planning and decision-making and by using a joint problem-solving approach to increase the chances of success. New initiatives will fail if insufficient time is given for people to explore both short-term practical and longer-term cultural issues. This requires considerable patience and long-term commitment on the part of those 'forcing' (Honey, 1997) the change(s). These characteristics are not present in the political arena where electoral cycles and demands can easily overtake and dictate 'top-down' changes. Currently, 'inclusion' is a watery concept, taking whatever shape is convenient to the perspective of diverse groups and individuals. Teachers, no longer 'enabled' to make significant decisions about the nature of the knowledge they impart or how to do this, have been led to expect more and more guidance. The roles and responsibilities of teachers in the classroom are being spelt out in ever more detail (e.g. TTA, 1999) but there is no definition as to what the 'authority' of the teacher is. This lack of definition has created further uncertainty among teachers. It has led them down a road leading to a state of de-professionalisation and dependency. They are now expected to embrace a creative and radical cultural change in attitude through behavioural 'indicators' and targets, a favourite of the rationalist empirical approach to learning and management (Bennett *et al.*, 1992).

Too much caution on the part of those releasing information or an over-weaning authoritative approach or too many 'top-down' initiatives, one after the other, can give *unexpected surprises* and trigger a great deal of unnecessary resistance. Fullan (1992) also warns that change cannot be forced from the top and that problems and questioning are inevitable and signs to be welcomed. Through engaging in the process of solving problems and in developing longer-term plans for schools and services, times of conflict, lack of enthusiasm and misunderstanding all form part of the process of attaining ownership and are thus part of the support needed during change. Even three-year development plans now become subject to interim changes of policy in Local Education Authorities. Teachers and head teachers are leaving the profession in droves due to increasing stress (through loss of control), workloads and the bruises from OfSTED inspections (TES, 2000). One of the consequences of rapid change and unexpected surprise is the loss of ability to participate and feel part of the process of change and development.

The concept of social inclusion challenges notions of 'normality' and 'averageness'. Yet the movement for testing, measuring attainment and target setting is based on a concept of averageness and so-called 'normal' attainment. There are such a wide range of pupils with diverse biological, social and emotional needs and disabilities that it is asking a great deal of teachers to be able to accommodate these needs within the narrow confines of the National Curriculum and a mainstream classroom. Is it possible to conceive of unilateral approaches that are effective? Particularly when concessions are not sufficiently made, for example, in making classes radically smaller. Is it satisfactory or even desirable, to have one type of institution for all? In order for a unified education system to cater for all of the diverse needs within it, it must be based on an ethos of flexibility and diversity of provision, on individual achievement, on personal progress and development. In other words, radical change in the education system as a whole is necessary and the teacher's role in making inclusion a possibility should be fully recognised. In order to avoid *unnecessary loss of routines* we need to build on the diversity of provision that has evolved; not try to go backwards, to remove existing systems and attempt to impose uniform provision.

The current push for inclusion comes on the back of many, many years of debate, ground-level initiatives and hard work. There is no need to attack the old in order to validate the new. This is not an 'honourable' way forward and can lead to considerable *loss of face* and harden patches of resistance. One of the problems with government statements on inclusion is the apparent assumption that all that is meant by inclusion is, *per se*, good, efficient and beneficial as an educational practice. This is far from proven and rests on an ideological plinth derived from a philosophy of 'human rights' and an emotive use of past negative examples of special schooling. This ignores the fact that it is essentially the same 'system' that has produced such exclusion and still does (Parsons, 1996). Special education in the 1970s was seen as supporting access and aiming to change the nature of education – making it truly liberal and broad. What has taken place is a *'colonisation, rather than a transformation of mainstream schooling'* (Dyson, 1997). The need for such segregation has arisen from a narrowly competitive, inflexible and middle-class education system. Not all of the evidence supports the idea that differentiation by school (or campus) is completely wrong educationally. For example, many girls do better academically in a single sex environment and many pupils with disabilities do just as well, if not better, in schools that specifically cater for some of their needs – usually their academic needs. So we have a situation where sociologically and politically it may have seemed appropriate to criticise special educators. However, including all pupils in an exclusive system is not yet proven to be the best way forward.

Care must be taken to include induction, training and other ways of dealing with *competence concerns* and developing new skills and understanding. Children do not fit into neat categories, nor do they conform exactly to diagnoses or sets of symptoms. For example, difficulties with behaviour are usually a complex interaction of biological, psychological and social factors (Cornwall, 1999). There is very rarely a simple, single solution to problems that are emotional or social in nature and that are serious enough to interfere significantly with learning. The label 'EBD' encompasses a wide range of biological, social and emotional conditions ranging from temporary disobedience through to the outward manifestation of more long-term mental health problems. It is difficult to conceive of unilateral approaches that could be effective. The reality is that teaching pupils with such a wide array of needs and capabilities is a highly skilled educational and teaching activity requiring considerable expertise. Schools, like many other organisations today, are still leaving the acquisition of the vital inter-personal skills (Furey, 1998) needed to promote inclusion, to chance. Providing opportunities for more, and better quality, long-term, accredited professional development is absolutely vital. Competence concerns constitute a significant barrier to teachers' commitment.

Change often produces consequences beyond its intended impact, or *ripple effects*. A sensitive manager or change agent will take the trouble to investigate as many of the consequences as possible prior to action or even discussion. The culture of 'focus group' consultation and political discussion aims to act as a filter, shaping the interpretation and negotiation of policy. The consequent impact is always relative. Individuals or groups do not have the same influence. For example, parents of average and achieving children are in the majority and can make their voice heard. It is this majority that will significantly influence the ethos of single mainstream schools. There are two groups who are not so able to influence policy. The first are the parents of children and young people in minority groups, whether learning, cultural, physical, social or emotional. The second group consists of practitioners themselves. They seem to attract very little attention and their views about education and diversity are seen to be unimportant. It is possible for ripple effects to build up into a tidal wave that could wash away the benefits of any given change.

The past ten years have seen the introduction of new legislation and statutory requirements in quantity and force, accompanied by negative comments from Her Majesty's Chief Inspector (HMCI) about teacher competence. Teachers and schools have changed to respond to these demands and teacher workloads have increased and changed in nature. The emphasis has moved from a basic concern with children with special educational needs (SEN), to how to conform to the bureaucratic paper requirements of monitoring and accountability. The push for conformity and bureaucracy involves *more and more work* and extra voluntary effort from teachers, not necessarily related to good educational practice. This is probably one of the major factors that cloud the perception of new initiatives (particularly if they are 'top-down'). The need for recognition of effort is universal and may act as a serious barrier to effective and lasting changes in culture.

Past resentments may well have been held for a long period of time. Without acknowledgement and some form of restorative action these may well carry fresh bitterness into a new situation. There is correlation between the persecution of failing schools by OfSTED (and some LEAs when it suits them), the identification of problem schools and pupils (often in the media) and the social or material deprivation of a significant number of pupils therein (Tomlinson, 2000). This correlation is so strong that it behoves us to question the ethics and sensibilities of the OfSTED machine and of those who manage our education system. This is directly antagonistic to the management of an inclusive education system. How can there be inclusion within an exclusive, competitive and elitist system that does not recognise the links between poverty, deprivation, social behaviour and learning difficulty? Children have become confined within a fundamentally alien and indifferent mainstream system (Dyson, 1997). A system that, subjected to an emphasis of despondency and criticism by media and politicians, has engendered much *loss of face* and now harbours many scars. Teachers contend daily with the negative cycle of conditioned failure and endure myths, reinforced by OfSTED, about the necessity for stigmatising failure in order to generate development. From generation to generation, these notions of 'failure' in education are perpetuated by the very institutions that advocate inclusion. The images of 'failure to make the grade' and 'failing schools', relentlessly thrown up by OfSTED, are seized upon by a hungry media. The potential impact of these past resentments is likely to be considerable.

If the changes are likely to cause *real threats* to people's livelihoods, status or quality of life then they should be 'opened up' as soon as possible. There is little advantage in 'dropping bombshells', causing resentment and damaging morale. The teaching profession should be classified as a 'professional bureaucracy' (Francis and Woodcock, 1987) characterised by a degree of creativity, autonomy in areas of professional implementation and self-reward from professional expertise and endeavour. It seems to have become a 'machine bureaucracy' (ibid.). Autonomous decisions are not encouraged. Deviations from strict requirements are punished. Conformity is encouraged and it is not necessary for employees to make decisions about the direction of their work or ultimate outcomes. The human element in planning and management, the 'enabling' qualities of management, have become lost in the bureaucratic rush to achieve targets in what might yet become another short-term political project. The current approach is one of 'rational epistemology' where 'knowledge' transcends individual human opinion and in which the state or church takes precedence (Kelly, 1995, p. 17). The real threat to teachers lies not just in being branded incompetent but that loss of earnings and employment are now linked to the requirement to conform to narrow, bureaucratic demands. The 'threat' is one of failure and this is not consistent with the longer-term development of a 'professional service' that will successfully include a diverse range of young people.

9.4   Just another 'cog' in the machine

Individual psychology recognises the many unique characteristics that each person brings to a situation. Both children and adults all respond differentially to new situations. The complexity of the change process requires considerable flexibility and responsiveness on the part of the teaching profession as a whole. Bureaucratic statistics may indicate patterns of social behaviour but the human factors involved make the prediction of individual behaviour impossible in any meaningful sense. Pupils themselves experience the consequences of educational management as a model of the authority of adults and social institutions. Young people are receiving messages of demand, conformity and acquiescence from educational institutions, not of exploration, learning and discovery. The culture of education management in past decades seems to be based on a classic orthodoxy of managerial organisation (Bennett *et al.*, 1992). It is a production line model where activities are broken down into their constituent parts in a linear fashion. The workers (teachers) are trained to carry out their specific tasks (curriculum 'delivery') and are thus 'atomised' into human machines. This machine-like quality in the system means that the work of schools has to be monitored in excessive detail, leading to excessive loss of (teaching and learning) routines. Whereas government and local authorities have previously required scientific rationality and quantitative data, now they are promoting an inclusive movement, generated by intuition and ideology and encouraged by an informal network of information. Inclusion, as much as anything, is about commitment, insight, community and acceptance, it is not about numbers and rationality. How can an educational administration concerned with the bureaucracy of targets, numbers and limited, but scientifically rational outcomes, be a part of this new equation?

During the 1980s and 1990s responsibilities and expectations levied onto schools and local education provision have been changing with increasing speed. It has been about power shifting to central government and local limited power to individual institutions, in contrast to Australia and New Zealand where it is largely about decentralisation:

Bennett *et al.*, 1992, p. 1

> 'Change is not just about the creation of new policies and procedures to implement external mandates. It is also about the development of personal strategies by individuals to respond to, and seek to influence the impact of, structural and cultural change: personal change as much as organisational change.'

Inclusion is about radical changes in the values, meanings and assumptions that exist in the education system. Education is already full of implicit assumptions about teaching. The OfSTED Frameworks and publications (1993, 1995a, 1995b, 1999a, 1999b and 2000), in seeking to define and control teaching and school management, are anonymously written and have no verifiable cultural provenance or research base. They have to be accepted with all their assumptions. At last, there has been some recognition of teachers' work (OfSTED, 1999b) and of the space, time, financial and human resources involved in working with children who have additional needs. Confident leadership with long-term vision should recognise the human effort and skills involved and allow its workforce to move forwards at a reasonable pace. It does not bode well that insecure leadership with an overactive tendency to impose and monitor in the finest detail seems to be the order of the day. Nevertheless, there have been some notable examples of progress and well-founded development in the UK (OfSTED, 1999b; TTA, 1999).

In the late 1980s, the conditions for facilitating the process of integration were analysed in detail and could still form a significant base for current practice. These encompassed the importance of teachers as enablers, along with a clear perception of related skills and knowledge, links between special and mainstream schools and the importance of supportive and facilitative management from LEAs (Hegarty and Moses, 1988; Jowett *et al.*, 1988; Moses *et al.*, 1988). Generally, it has been a patchy process and an uphill struggle in the face of aggressive and almost militant educational legislation and policy. Explicit strategies and statements have expressed a desire to flush out the 'cancer' in the teaching profession and blamed teachers for the lack of ability to cope with politicised educational demands. Political posturing has interfered enormously in the teaching profession but has never accepted any responsibility when the results of this insecure and unpredictable 'management style' go drastically wrong.

9.5 No more 'turning schools around'

Bennett *et al.*, (1992) sum up the conflicting forces at work very effectively in two models of management at opposite ends of a spectrum. The 'rational' model is characterised by control, segmentation and adherence to the 'one best way' of doing things. This produces a language of control and command. The second is characterised by shared commitment, empowerment of the work force and delegation (to well trained and responsible professionals) with authority and status. In moulding these two models together, there is the implication that those in authority have the same interests at heart as those delivering the goods. This cannot be assumed to be true. The 'goods' in this case are the 'curriculum' and 'results'. Educational change is 'technically simple but socially complex' (Fullan, 1992) and because change is a learning experience for those involved in its implementation, it is often the 'science of muddling through' (Lindblom, 1959). Lindblom asserts that because change forces a challenge to the individual's assumptive world at work, implementation may require authority *in the first instance*, rather than consent. This is the model of 'top-down' change that has become manipulation by a series of '*in the first instances*' for the past two decades, a kind of 'death by innovation'.

Current policy does not go far enough, new developments in ICT, individual empowerment and learning theory look likely to outstrip the current manipulative and static notions of inclusion in practice. They are likely to produce so many ripple effects that current fixed and institutionalised notions of inclusion will very soon be outdated and useless. The provision of a greater variety of smaller and smaller, more flexible centres of education look far more interesting and grass-roots initiatives have shown them to be effective and enticing. If 'Excellence for all' is to be a workable, if flawed, idea, there needs to be a greater diversity of educational goals and facilities or provision; not rendering down the variety of approaches and areas of knowledge into one large and all-encompassing educational factory or retro-institution. It has been argued in this chapter that the education system itself is inherently exclusive and that managing change to produce responsible inclusion should first be looking at the visions and messages communicated 'from the top' and the way that the system itself is traditionally 'exclusive'. The time for 'turning schools around' has come to an end and it is now time to 'turn the policies around' and change the culture of education itself. It is time to do the following:

◆ develop a more participative view of human resource management and change the very hierarchical and outdated nature of educational management into a more collegiate system;
◆ enhance the flexibility and authority of teachers by giving them better professional development opportunities and status – a major curriculum and management reform driven locally by teachers themselves;
◆ develop a longer-term focus on what is educational and a positive, liberal view of education to deal with short-term uncertainty caused by conformity to rigid rules and fear of failure;

◆ engage in a gradual process of radical change in the way the education service is delivered in order to make it 'inclusive', preceded by a significant period of discussion and led by in-school initiatives;

◆ develop partnerships and teamwork in schools and between community services and schools, crossing 'functional areas' and 'professional barriers' to provide a coherent and consistent service to pupils and parents;

◆ disband OfSTED inspections and any remnants of the 'culture of failure and elitism' that has grown up in the education system;

◆ change the accountability emphasis so that teachers and schools will no longer be directed in terms of what is taught, and how, but be accountable in terms of their professional and educational aims;

◆ recognise teachers as autonomous professionals who are able to make good decisions based on their 'would be' excellent training and continuing professional development opportunities.

9.6　Conclusion

Inclusion is a radical process of change – not just tinkering with behaviours and targets, generating bureaucratic leverage or changing the scope and size of educational institutions and moving children about in them or between them. The successive years of wearing down the teaching profession have rested on a series of aggressive programmes: highlighting weaknesses; exposing schools to negative media attention; undermining teachers' professional standing and professionalism by turning them into mechanistic 'deliverers'; and limiting the definition of appropriate knowledge. It is not surprising therefore that the seed bed for change is stony ground and that the management of change has not recognised the importance and quality of individual teachers in the workforce. In fact, the introduction of divisive performance-related pay structures puts teachers on the level of 'piece workers', unlike other professionals such as doctors, lawyers and health workers. The emphasis throughout the past two decades on the 'task', sometimes on the group but generally to the detriment of the individual is a very shaky foundation. This chapter has developed the general hypothesis that the management of change within the public education system in the United Kingdom has not been undertaken responsibly. There is no reason to believe that further developments in the process of 'inclusion' will be any different and we should heed the words of Kanter (cited in McCalman and Paton, 1992): *'everyone is going to compete for people in the 1990s. In fact, the quality of people is going to make a bigger difference than the quality of products or the quality of services.'*

It appears that there is something of a crisis of recruitment looming within the public education system (TES, 2000) and perhaps these words should have been heeded during the 1990s when the opportunities to change the way the system was managed presented themselves.

It is important that we revisit the 'management of change' in education over the past two decades because we are in danger of continuing to apply tired old solutions to new and increasingly challenging problems. These challenges will stem more and more from the advances in culture, science and technology that are outstripping our social and educational institutions. It is too easy to criticise the 'change masters' who are generating massive amounts of paper guidance and setting targets. A ready acknowledgement of the human impact of changes in the public education system, and the time needed to make them work, would be helpful. At national and local levels, politicians and local authority executives are, on the one hand, ambiguous about what inclusion means and, on the other, concerned with their own agendas, including over-rapid consultation and action. The imposition of change in education seems to have become a political tradition. The initial authority required to generate change has become a form of oppression in itself. How can a system of educational management from the political sphere to local and regional executives, pretend to purvey a culture of inclusion when the very means by which the change is wrought, is exclusive within an exclusive system? Thank goodness inclusion is really about people in their communities and relationships, not about political accomplishment and social engineering.

References

Bennett, N., Crawford, M. and Riches, C. (eds) *Managing Change in Education: Individual and Organizational Perspectives*, London, Paul Chapman, 1992.

Bevington, J. 'Cognitive management: using Beck's model of emotional disorders to facilitate change within organisations' *The Occupational Psychologist* 37 (3), 1999, pp. 3–6.

Booth, T., Ainscow, M., Black-Hawkins, K., Vaughan, M. and Shaw, L. *The Index of Inclusion: Developing Learning and Participation in Schools*, London, Centre for Studies on Inclusive Education, 2000.

Booth, T., Ainscow, M. and Dyson, A. 'England: inclusion and exclusion in a competitive system', in *From Them to Us: An International Study of Inclusion in Education*, T. Booth and M. Ainscow (eds), London, Routledge, 1998.

Brown, S. *Equity: Keeping it in the Forefront of Educational Thinking for the Future*, keynote address to the FORUM on Educational Research in Edinburgh, 16 May, 1997.

Cornwall, J. *Choice, Opportunity and Learning: Educating Children and Young People Who Are Disabled*, London, David Fulton, 1995.

Cornwall, J. 'Pressure, stress and children's behaviour at school', in *Young Children Learning*, T. David (ed.), London, Paul Chapman, 1999.

Department for Education and Employment *Excellence for All Children: Meeting Special Educational Needs*, London, HMSO, 1997.

Department for Education and Employment *Meeting Special Educational Needs: A Programme of Action*, Sudbury, DfEE Publications, 1998.

Dyson, A. 'Social and educational disadvantage: reconnecting special needs education', *British Journal of Special Education* 24 (4), 1997, pp. 152–6.

Francis, D. and Woodcock, M. *People at Work: A Practical Guide to Organizational Change*, La Jolla, CA, University Associates, 1987.

Fullan, M. *Successful School Improvement: The Implementation Perspective and Beyond*, Milton Keynes, Open University Press, 1992.

Furey, P. 'Interpersonal skills coaching for business: evaluation of a brief training approach', *The Occupational Psychologist* 3 (13), 1998, pp. 3–13.

Gergen, K. 'Beyond the self–society antimony', *Journal of Constructivist Psychology* 12, 1999, pp. 173–8.

Goldstein, H. *Social Learning and Change: A Cognitive Approach to Human Services,* London, Tavistock Publications, 1984.

Hegarty, S. and Moses, D. (eds) *Developing Expertise: INSET for Special Educational Needs*, Berkshire, NFER-Nelson, 1988.

Honey, P. *Improve Your People Skills*. 2nd edition. London, Institute of Personnel and Development, 1997.

Jowett, S., Hegarty, S. and Moses, D. *Joining Forces: A Study of Links between Special and Ordinary Schools*, Berkshire, NFER-Nelson, 1988.

Kanter, R. *The Change Masters*, London, Routledge, 1984.

Kanter, R. *'Managing Change – The Human Dimension'*, Creativity and Innovation Yearbook, vol. 1, Manchester, Business School, 1988.

Kanter, R. *When Giants Learn to Dance: Mastering the Challenges of Strategy, Management and Careers in the 1990s*, London, Unwin Hayman, 1989.

Kelly, A.V. *Education and Democracy: Principles and Practice*, London, Paul Chapman, 1995.

Kelly, G. *The Psychology of Personal Constructs*, New York, Van Nostrand, 1955.

Lindblom, C. ' The science of muddling through', *Public Administration Review* 19, 1959, pp. 155–69.

Lunt, I. 'A chance for change?', *Special!* Summer, 1998, pp. 24–5.

McCalman, J. and Paton, R. *Change Management: A Guide to Effective Implementation*, London, Paul Chapman, 1992.

Moses, D., Hegarty, S. and Jowett, S. *Supporting Ordinary Schools: LEA Initiatives*, Berkshire, NFER-Nelson, 1998.

Office for Standards in Education *Handbook for the Inspection of Schools*, London, HMSO, 1993.

Office for Standards in Education *Guidance on the Inspection of Nursery and Primary Schools*, London, HMSO, 1995a.

Office for Standards in Education *Guidance on the Inspection of Special Schools*, London, HMSO, 1995b.

Office for Standards in Education '*Educational inclusion and school inspection: briefing for inspectors, inspection providers and schools*', from *Inspecting Schools*, London, TSO, 1999a.

Office for Standards in Education *Special Education 1994–98: A Review of Special Schools, Secure Units and Pupil Referral Units in England*, London, TSO, 1999b.

Office for Standards in Education *Handbook for Inspecting Special Schools and Pupil Referral Units – with guidance on self-evaluation*, London, TSO, 2000.

Parsons, C. 'Permanent exclusions from school: a case where society is failing its children', *Support for Learning* 11 (3), 1996, pp. 109–12.

Pheysey, D. *Organisational Cultures*, London, Routledge, 1993.

Smith, M. *Social Science in Question*, London, Sage Publications in association with The Open University, 1998.

Stam, H. 'Personal construct theory and social constructionism: difference and dialogue', *Journal of Constructivist Psychology* 11, 1998, pp. 187–203.

Times Educational Supplement 'Threshold fails to stem staff exodus', 23 June, 2000, pp. 1–2.

Tomlinson, S. *Critical Issues in Inclusion and Exclusion*, Keynote speaker. Seminar at Canterbury Christ Church University College, May, 2000.

Teacher Training Agency *National Special Educational Needs Specialist Standards*, London, TTA, 1999.

Wallace, M. and McMahon, A. *Planning for Change in Turbulent Times*, London, Cassell, 1994.

Walsh, S. 'Adapting cognitive analytic therapy to make sense of harmful work environments', *British Journal of Medical Psychology* 69 (3), 1996, p. 20.

Chapter 10 — Inclusion: A developmental perspective

Sue Pearson

10.1 Introduction

The shift towards inclusion is clearly more than simply a 'linguistic adjustment' (Slee, 1998) and it is much more appropriately perceived as a shift of culture (Corbett, 1999). However, language and culture are inter-related since language is an 'artefact of culture'. In this chapter, the metaphor of language development is used to explore the issues related to the development of inclusive education.

A substantial body of research exists in relation to language development. Evidence has shown that humans are born with a *predisposition* to learn language (Lenneberg, 1967) and individual differences occur based on genetics, culture and social factors (Martin and Miller, 1999). It is also accepted that language development follows predetermined stages (Brown, 1973).

Language use is frequently analysed under three headings: form, content and use (Bloom and Lahey, 1978). Content, often referred to as *semantics*, relates to the study of meaning and relationships between meanings. Users are able to operate effectively in a system where one particular word may carry multiple meanings where they rely on the context to decide which of the meanings is intended. For example, multiple meanings of the word 'right' exist. *Pragmatics* is concerned with the use of language in context, by real speakers and real hearers in real situations, and relates to an utterance having a force beyond the face value of the linguistic information because of the speaker–hearer context. A single word utterance of 'right' can convey many meanings determined by the purpose and intent of the speaker: question, affirmation, direction, irony.

For each person, the *development of language* takes place well into adult life and perhaps never ceases. The evidence seems to suggest that language development in individuals follows a range of pre-determined stages although there are significant variations in when particular individuals reach specific stages culminating in the ability to deal effectively with a complex and dynamic system. In addition to individuals developing language, language itself also *evolves* over time so that word use and word meaning can change over time. Language is an open-ended system where change is to be anticipated although the exact changes are unpredictable.

10.2 Predisposition

The evidence from Ward and Le Dean (1996) indicates a positive disposition exists within the teaching profession towards the ideal of inclusion. Norwich (2000a) uses his study in relation to integration to indicate a more complex picture.

> *'In both samples, over 90% of teachers agreed with the statement that "Integration is a desirable educational practice" with about 60% agreeing strongly. However when the focus becomes more specific the degree of endorsement decreased. In response to the statement "All have the right to be in ordinary classrooms" just under 70% agreed and only 30% agreed strongly. Disagreement to this statement rose to 20%. In response to a statement about feasibility the agreement dropped more sharply.'*

2000, p. 12

The predisposition among others in the inclusion debate, such as parents and pupils, may be even more complex. Allan (1999) provides a useful insight into the issues related to pupils both those with special educational needs (SEN) and their mainstream peers. She tellingly refers to mainstream pupils as 'inclusion gatekeepers' who demonstrate a degree of ambiguity in relation to pupils with SEN.

> *'Their governmental regime, with its pastoral and pedagogical features, seemed mostly to support and guide the inclusion of pupils with special needs and enabled some of the conventional rules between pupils to be broken. But the regime also legitimised the exclusion of some pupils.'*

1999, p. 44

Within the literature, there are many examples of the enthusiasm of parents of children with SEN for inclusive practice although this is not true for all parents of pupils with SEN (Thomas and Dwyfor Davies, 1999). With some notable exceptions (Lewis, 1995), there is less evidence about the views of other parents. It would appear that for them there is the full spread of views along a continuum (Thomas *et al.*, 1998).

Humans are born with a predisposition to learn language but research has suggested that early experiences influence the extent to which this predisposition is deployed. In terms of inclusion, it seems critically important to recognise that there are great variations in people's attitude to inclusion and that there exists a potential to modify those views. The focus needs to be on encouraging positive dispositions – and it may be that legislation alone is insufficient.

10.3   Semantics

10.3.1 Synonyms?

Historically, in the debate about the restructuring of provision two terms have been used – integration and inclusion. While some authors use these interchangeably, the majority see them as being discrete ideas (Florian, 1998a, 1998b; Corbett, 1998; Norwich, 2000b). Yet, because there are multiple understandings of both integration and inclusion, determining the distinction between the two can be problematic. However, there does appear to be a consensus that it relates to the degree of involvement in change of the various parties. In integration, the onus for change is on those with special educational needs whereas inclusion involves a redefining of patterns and conditions (Florian, 1998a).

10.3.2 Homonym or polyseme?

A homonym is a word that has more than one unrelated meaning such as 'fan' – a device for moving air or an admirer. They appear as separate dictionary entries. A polyseme is a word that can have more than one related meaning such as the example of 'mouth' – entrance to a cave, opening in the face, estuary. They appear under one dictionary entry. The decisions are to some extent arbitrary and may be lost in history.

'Inclusion' certainly has multiple meanings. The term is used at both the macro and the micro level (Norwich, 2000b) and in relation to both social changes and educational changes. The term is used in a range of inter-related discourses: medical discourse, charity discourse, rights' discourse, lay and corporate discourses, market discourse and most recently aesthetic discourse (Allan, 1999). Dyson (2000) attempted to illustrate the inter-relatedness of the discourses by suggesting that they can be grouped along two inter-related continuums, one focusing on the rationale for inclusion and one on realisation. This can then represent:

- ◆ the rationale for inclusion: the rights and ethics discourse;
- ◆ the rationale for inclusion: the efficacy discourse;
- ◆ the realisation of inclusive education: the political discourse;
- ◆ the realisation of inclusive education: the pragmatic discourse.

Dyson raises, and then largely rebuts, the suggestions that the ambiguities surrounding inclusion are such that it might be more appropriate to talk about 'inclusions'. A drift too far in this direction would almost certainly be unhelpful since it would legitimise each 'inclusion' accruing a literature and research base of its own and as Booth (1998, p. 88) comments: *'People specialise in smaller and smaller areas of the literature and are hence oblivious to the connection of their ideas to the ideas of others.'*

Perhaps the route forward, at this stage of the development of inclusive education, is to treat all the various meanings of inclusion as polysemes, with related meanings, but then to explore the relationships between the various meanings. However, the continued absence of a single agreed definition places the onus on readers to ensure that they contextualise the use of the word 'inclusion' and understand the meaning prescribed by the author (Booth, 1998). In this way the lack of consistency does not pose a threat to the whole inclusive education movement (Feiler and Gibson, 1999).

10.3.3 Classifying inclusion

In an attempt to provide greater clarity some authors have provided 'classifications of inclusion'. Farrell (2000) uses the categories full, mainstream and educational inclusion while Corbett (1999) adopts the categories of surface, structural and deep inclusion. Levels of inclusiveness in different countries have been compared using terms such as 'limited', 'emerging', 'segregated', 'approaching' and finally integrated. (Mazuerk and Winzer, cited in Corbett, 1998). There is a danger that value judgements may be inferred from some of the terms used that may prove unhelpful. Additionally, none of these classifications are particularly illuminating unless the reader has understood the meaning of 'inclusion' as prescribed by the author. These terms superficially appear to be more descriptive. Real opportunities exist for differences to exist between intended and perceived meanings.

10.3.4 Lack of a shared understanding

An unintentional outcome of this complexity of language and concepts is that establishing a shared understanding of inclusion is elusive. Additionally, cross-referencing of the research and practice becomes extremely problematic. Does the innovation in one setting that is being described as 'inclusive' meet the criteria for inclusion as promulgated elsewhere? As Feiler and Gibson comment:

'Inclusion in practice is a very complex area that requires a detailed and precise definition, for otherwise, there is a danger that schools can claim that their provision is inclusive when the opposite may well be the case.'

1999, p. 148

It may be some time, if ever, before such a precise definition is available. In the meantime, authors are not always explicit about the definition of inclusion that they have prescribed. Therefore, it is critically important that in reading the literature, readers make every effort to be clear about the definition that the author is using and to take this into account.

10.3.5 Pragmatics

Individuals use contextual clues to determine the meaning ascribed to communication, even single word utterances. It is entirely possible for two individuals with significantly different backgrounds to access the same material and reach very different conclusions. In this situation, misconceptions and misunderstanding can arise. Norwich (2000b) draws attention to the types of difficulties that can occur when joint understandings do not exist. Perhaps this example is the tip of a much greater iceberg where the intended meaning is not the same as the received meaning.

10.3.6 Intention of the author

In my comments on language development, attention was drawn to the way in which single word utterances can have varied meanings. Consider the potential meanings of 'Yes'. The authors of material on inclusion come from a range of diverse and disparate backgrounds and their motivations for writing are very different. The result is that the literature surrounding inclusion ranges through the emotive using terms such as 'appeasement' (Ainscow *et al.*, 2000), the purely ideological, personal autobiographies, to academic debates. Again, the onus is on the reader to have an awareness of the author and their intentions.

10.4 Development process of inclusion

Some of the tensions in defining and understanding inclusion have been identified. Despite these complexities, it is clear that practice is changing. A considerable body of literature is gathering around the topic of inclusion. This tends to focus on shifts in educational practice and employs the model relevant to that field of study. However, it is also fundamentally about change, whether this is at a societal, organisational, group or individual level; and a realignment of grouping.

Inclusion is about developing a new culture and as such involves new social groupings or existing groupings operating in different ways. This applies at all levels including:

◆ pupil–pupil relationships;
◆ pupil–teacher relationships;
◆ teacher–teacher relationships;
◆ teachers and Learning Support Assistant (LSA);
◆ LSA and pupils;
◆ other agencies–teacher relationships;
◆ support staff–other teachers.

In many of the accounts, the significance of relationships is referred to. For example, Thomas *et al*. (1998) note that

'The success of inclusion (as distinct from integration) depends crucially on how teaching is organised and how <u>interaction</u> among pupils is structured and helped.'

1998, p. 47

'The arrangements in which teachers and learning support assistants are finding themselves in inclusive classrooms mean involvement in <u>teamwork</u>, but good teamwork is notoriously difficult to achieve.'

1998, p. 26   (emphasis added)

The reformulating of social groupings, regardless of the vision of inclusion they are working towards, appears to be significant and worthy of consideration in its own right. At the level of staff, despite all the apparent enthusiasm for greater collaboration, the reality remains difficult to achieve. Lacey (2000) and Thomas *et al*. (1998) provide an overview of the evidence about friendship groups and peer interaction.

Chapman and Ware (1999) applied a modified version of the model of Tuckman *et al*. (1997) – forming, storming, norming and performing – to their experience of developing multidisciplinary practice as a response to pupils being located in more inclusive settings. The model, set out in Figure 10.1, may have an application to the realignments that are occurring more generally. If the proposition that the shift towards inclusion, at whatever level, is related to group processes then it ought to be possible to demonstrate that this model is applicable and relevant and could ideally offer fresh insights.

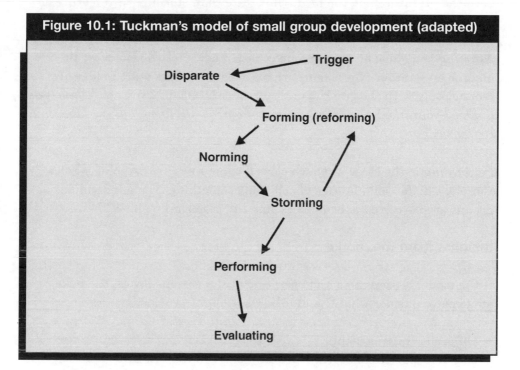

Figure 10.1: Tuckman's model of small group development (adapted)

Disparate is not used pejoratively but reflects the reality that alternative social groupings exist prior to forming. In the case of special education, a number of authors have drawn attention to the separate systems, policies and practices that exist prior to any move towards inclusion. Disparate can equally be applied to the individuals involved. For example, there was a stage during which it was unusual for teachers from special schools to work with mainstream colleagues. Even where expertise has been developed in group work, the move towards inclusive practice may alter the participants. For example, therapists had established roles when working with teaching colleagues in special schools, the move towards more inclusive practice involves them in working with a new range of colleagues (Chapman and Ware, 1999).

Forming is a stage at which there is considerable anxiety, relationships are tested, dependency on the leader and some attempts to define the group. Clearly, new groupings are being forged at all levels (Bannister *et al.*, 1998; Chapman and Ware, 1999). Indeed, some would link inclusion to the building of a new structure in society.

Storming is a stage at which conflict emerges between the sub-groups. Defensiveness, competitiveness and jealousy accompany it. Reference to both the literature and the media illustrate that 'storming' is a feature of the changes.

Norming is a stage at which group cohesion develops. Norms start to emerge and authority problems are resolved. Members start to identify more closely with the group. Bannister *et al.* (1998, p. 68) state: *'Discuss as a school your ideals. Not everyone might agree with them, but try to reach a consensus.'*

Performing is the stage at which clear flexible roles are established and there is satisfaction in terms of achieving something. Some individuals or groups are perceived to be approaching the performing phase.

10.5 Insights from the model

If the model is applicable and operating at the various levels, the next stage is to consider what useful insights it might provide:

◆ Different starting points.
◆ Different participants will react differently to the 'triggers'.
◆ Turbulence will be part of the process.
◆ There are no instant answers.
◆ There will be a succession of stages in the move towards more inclusive practice.
◆ Short cuts may be inefficient.
◆ Support through the process of change may be essential.
◆ Energy will both be needed and created in the process of change.
◆ Tensions arise when different parties are at different stages of the cycle.
◆ Tensions will arise when there are either different expectations of the pace of change or there are in reality differences in pace.
◆ New 'final' groupings may require new skills before they can become effective.

Different starting points. What is entirely clear is that different schools, authorities and individuals have very different starting points. The move from an integrated setting to an inclusive one is not the same as a segregated system moving towards an inclusive system. Each individual has their own history and experiences that will influence their reaction to and progress towards more inclusive practice. Predisposition and prior experiences are significant.

Different participants will react differently to the 'triggers'. A variety of 'triggers' are currently being employed to bring about a shift towards inclusive practice. These include government policy and advice, local authority policy and advice, exhortation from various groupings, advocacy by individual or groups and examples of 'good practice' being publicised. It does seem reasonable to suggest that the nature of the trigger will have long-term consequences. If purely legislative means are used, a form of 'contrived collegiality' (Hargreaves, 1992) may be established rather than the more desirable 'collaborative culture'. What is striking in the literature reporting shifts towards more inclusive practice is how often the trigger has either been the passionate commitment of an individual or group of individuals or the opportunity for change exists and the move towards inclusion being the selected direction. This is in line with the evidence of Hopkins (1994) that school improvement is more likely to occur if it is driven from within the organisation. Neither the issue of 'heart and minds' nor opportunism should be overlooked. For example, with reference to schools, Hargreaves (1999) suggests it is unsafe to assume:

> *'that the staff will be persuaded, on some kind of rationale basis, to shed older beliefs, attitudes and values under the spell of the new ones offered by the leader's stated vision. In reality, most people's beliefs, attitudes and values are far more resistant to change than leaders typically allow, and direct attempts to change them may stimulate increased resistance.'*

1999, p. 59

Turbulence will be part of the process. The evidence seems to suggest that there are periods of turbulence during the process of change. Some of these are related to tensions between people's views of inclusion, some the natural accompaniment of change and other instances will be a consequence of being involved in the alignment of groupings that is taking place. Those responsible for managing the change need to consider the causes of any turbulence

There are no instant answers. The theory of group dynamics suggests that the development of effective and efficient new groupings does take time.

There will be a succession of stages in the move towards more inclusive practice. Commentaries about shifts in practice do seem to indicate a shift through various stages, however loosely defined these are. Moore *et al.* (1987), cited in Thomas (1998), note the stages a link scheme had to work through before interaction could take place. Johnstone and Warwick (1999) report on two schools that felt they had reached the stage where staff throughout the school were confident enough to take responsibility for the learning of all pupils. There may not be a neat linear progress but may be a rather more complex pattern of progress. There may be transitional phases and indeed some authors have suggested that inclusion is an unattainable ideal.

An implication of this is that judgements about schools and individuals should be based on 'shift towards inclusion' rather than absolute judgements. Corbett (1999) illustrates this point in reference to a child who is very withdrawn and refuses to speak in class who eventually, through stages, starts to communicate. If only the end point is judged, for example by external measures, the significance and value of the shift may be overlooked.

Short cuts may be inefficient. This model proposes that there are stages to be worked through to bring about the transformation. Initiatives that do not recognise and try to take 'short cuts' may be counterproductive. Johnstone and Warwick (1999) imply that the two schools they describe did not change their practice until they were confident that *all* staff were ready. This is very different to the situation where a school, which is struggling to provide an inclusive ethos for those already in the school, feels an external pressure to cater for a more diverse group of pupils. There is an issue about pace and timing. As Slee cautions:

> '*Reform needs to take the long-term view. This proposition proceeds from a sense of profound crisis. The crisis is uneven in its impacts. Its depth is seen in relation to specific areas of disadvantage and privilege. For many, the crisis of schooling is personalised and restricted to a private struggle. Is there any sense including people in schools that are not working for many of the students already there?*'

1999, p. 204

Support through the process of change may be essential. In education, where there is a long tradition of applying this model of group formation, there is recognition of the need to support the creation and effective functioning of groups. Indeed, in the case of staff, a need and desire for support given the recruitment onto courses relating to inclusion exist. It is not simply a matter of quantity but also quality. The significance of group relationships is again raised when Johnstone and Warwick comment:

> *'In our experience, support staff have found that participating in the group offers more valuable training than accredited courses at the local education development centre or open university courses. Personal contact, hands-on experiences and regular meetings provide opportunities to learn together.'*
>
> 1999, p. 108

Energy will both be needed and created in the process of change. The evidence is that the formation of new groupings absorbs energy but that it may also release and create energy. Some of the literature discusses at length the resource implications of inclusion but this clearly identifies the resource implications of bringing about the transformation. As Corbett (1999, p. 129) comments in relation to her examination of integration over the last fifteen years: *'the individuals being integrated are expected to have reserves of courage and tenacity well beyond what could usually be considered reasonable to expect.'* This model suggests that there may need to be short-term investment to facilitate change and ultimately release new energies.

Tensions arise when different parties are at different stages of the cycle. This can be illustrated at the micro level by reference to families who are at the performing stage when they are confronted by schools that may be at an earlier stage in the cycle. Similarly, schools are faced by dilemmas since various parts of the education system are at different stages of the cycle. One part of the system is attempting to trigger more inclusive practices while schools are expected to be at a performing stage in which they produce ever improving GCSE grades.

While in the medium to long term these aims may not be incompatible, in the short term, individuals and schools are faced with real dilemmas about which initiative, which directive to give priority to and therefore in which direction to shift the culture. For example, in reference to social inclusion, Gray and Panter (2000, p. 7) comment: *'Many teachers and schools that might have been more committed to persevering with difficult pupils have found it more difficult to do so, for fear that they will be negatively judged.'* While it is inevitable that there will be different cycles operating at society level, at school level, at individual level.

Tensions will arise when there are either different expectations of the pace of change or there are in reality differences in pace. The notion that shifts towards inclusive practice are long-term reforms has been introduced earlier. Some lobby groups appear to wish for changes to occur very rapidly and while this is entirely understandable, it may, at least, in the short term be counter-productive. Ball (1999) describes how a group was established eighteen months before the date two children with disabilities moved to a school for pupils aged thirteen to eighteen. That time not only allowed the buildings to be adapted but also for attitudes towards inclusion to become more positive. The parents, pupils and schools appear to have recognised the need for time and to have worked to an agreed agenda. Where such agreement does not exist and a child placement in a new setting occurs prior to that setting, preparing to meet the child's needs in what was intended to be a more inclusive setting may, in fact, be more excluding. The provision superficially may represent more inclusive practice, it unintentionally produces the opposite effect. This has been referred to as 'maindumping'.

At another level, tensions arise when there exists, educationally, an enthusiasm for and opportunity for more inclusive practice but the financial structures are more slowly shifting from those that support segregated practice.

New 'final' groupings may require new skills before they can become effective. A recurrent theme in the literature is for in-service to support change. This also applies to Initial Teacher Education.

The move towards more inclusive practice is without question an educational change but it also involves new groups forming or existing groupings being modified. Lack of attention to this aspect will detract from the whole enterprise.

So far the metaphor has been linked to how individuals develop their language. But language itself is not static – it evolves over time. One of the reasons for this is that the culture in which it is embedded evolves. Recent developments in technology have widened the vocabulary that we use and some words accrue meanings beyond their original ones. In the same way, understandings of inclusion will shift both as the term itself is refined and as societal changes occur.

10.6 Conclusion

A generally agreed definition of inclusion does not yet exist – and, indeed, may never do so. But that lack of agreement does not inhibit the encouragement to change practice or deter changes in practice. It does, however, mean that anyone considering this area needs to do the following:

◆ recognise the predisposition of all those involved and reflect the belief that these are open to change;
◆ clarify the prescribed meaning of words used and do not assume an automatic joint understanding;
◆ contextualise the comments so that not only the meaning but the intention are explicit;
◆ recognise that moves in relation to inclusion involve re-alignment of groupings and that this is a process in its own right;
◆ anticipate that meanings will change over time both as the meanings are clarified but also as society and school change.

This may sound a daunting agenda, yet, to return to the original metaphor, sophisticated language users not only tolerate a diversity of language but also actively engage with its subtleties. The same sophisticated approach needs to be adopted by educators so that they can apply 'innovative thinking' (Hart, 1996) to inclusion.

References

Ainscow, M., Black-Hawkins, K., Vaughan, M. and Shaw, L. (Centre for Studies on Inclusive Education) *Index for Inclusion: Developing, Learning and Participation in Schools*, Bristol, CSIE, 2000.

Allan, J. *Actively Seeking Inclusion: Pupils with Special Needs in Mainstream Schools*, London, Falmer Press, 1999.

Ball, M. *School Inclusion: The School, the Family and the Community*, York, Joseph Rowntree Foundation, 1999.

Bannister, C., Sharland, V., Thomas G., Upton, V. and Walker, D. 'Changing from a special school to an inclusive service', *British Journal of Special Education* 25 (2), 1998, pp. 65–9.

Bloom, L. and Lahey, M. *Language Development and Language Disorders*, New York, Wiley, 1978.

Booth, T. 'The poverty of special education' in *Theorising Special Education*, C. Clark, A. Dyson and A. Millward (eds) London, Routledge, 1998.

Brown, R. *A First Language: The Early Stages*, Cambridge, MA, Harvard University Press, 1973.

Chapman, L. and Ware, J. 'Challenging traditional roles and perception: using transdisciplinary approach in a mainstream school', *Support for Learning* 14 (3), 1999, pp. 104–9.

Corbett, J. *Special Educational Needs in the Twentieth Century: A Cultural Analysis,* London, Cassell, 1998.

Corbett, J. 'Inclusivitiy and school culture: the case for special education' in *School Culture*, J. Prosser (ed.) London, Paul Chapman Publishing, 1999.

Department for Education and Employment *Excellence for All Children: Meeting Special Educational Needs*, London, DfEE, 1997.

Dyson, A. 'Question, understanding and supporting the inclusive school', in *Special Education Reformed: Beyond the Rhetoric?,* H. Daniels, (ed.), London, Falmer Press, 2000.

Farrell, M. 'Educational inclusion and raising standards', *British Journal of Special Education* 27 (1), 2000, pp. 35–8.

Feiler, A. and Gibson, H. 'Threats to the inclusive movement', *British Journal of Special Education* 26 (3), 1999, pp. 147–52.

Florian, L. 'Inclusive practice: what, why and how?', in *Promoting Inclusive Practice*, C. Tilstone, L. Florian and R. Rose (eds), London, Routledge, 1998a.

Florian, L. 'An examination of the practical problems associated with the implementation of inclusive educational policies', *Support for Learning* 13 (3), 1998b, pp. 105–98.

Gray, P. and Panter, S. 'Exclusion or inclusion? A perspective on policy in England for pupils with emotional and behavioural difficulties', *Support for Learning* 15 (1), 2000, pp. 4–7

Hargreaves, A. 'Cultures of teaching: a focus for change', in *Understanding Teacher Development*, A. Hargreaves and M.G. Fullan (eds), London, Cassell, 1992.

Hargreaves, A. 'Helping practitioners explore their school culture', in *School Culture*, J. Prosser (ed.) London, Paul Chapman, 1999.

Hart, S. *Beyond Special Needs: Enhancing Children's Learning through Innovative Thinking*, London, Paul Chapman Publishing, 1996.

Hopkins, D. 'The Yellow Brick Road', *Managing Schools Today* 3, 1994, pp. 14–7.

Johnstone, D. and Warwick, C. 'Community solutions to inclusion: some observation on practice in Europe and the United Kingdom', *Support for Learning* 14 (1), 1999, pp. 8–12.

Lacey, P. 'Multidisciplinary work', in *Special Education Reformed: Beyond rhetoric?,* H. Daniels, (ed.), London, Falmer Press, 2000.

Lenneberg, E.H. *Biological Foundations of Language*, New York, Wiley, 1967.

Lewis, A. *Children's Understanding of Disability*, London, Routledge, 1995.

Martin, D. and Miller, C. *Language and the Curriculum: Practitioner Research in Planning Differentiation*, London, David Fulton, 1999.

Mazurek, K. and Winzer, M. (eds) *Comparative Studies in Special Education*, Washington, DC, Gallandet University Press, 1994.

Moore, J., Carpenter, B. and Lewis, A. '"He can really do it!": an account of partial integration in a first (5–8) school', *Education* 3 (13), 1987, pp. 37–43.

Norwich, B. 'The withdrawal of inclusion 1996–98: a continuing trend', *British Journal of Special Education* 27 (1), 2000a, pp. 39–40.

Norwich, B 'Inclusion in education: from concepts, values and critique to practice', in *Special Education Reformed: Beyond Rhetoric?*, H. Daniels (ed.), London, Falmer Press, 2000b.

Rose, R., Fletcher, W. and Goodwin, G. 'Pupils with severe learning difficulties as personal target setters', *British Journal of Special Education* 26 (4), 1999, pp. 206–13.

Slee, R. 'The politics of special education' in *Theorising Special Education*, C. Clark, A. Dyson and A. Millward (eds), London, Routledge, 1998.

Slee, R. 'Policies and practices? Inclusive education and its effects on schooling', in *Inclusive Education*, H. Daniels and P. Garner (eds), London, Kogan Page, 1999.

Thomas, G. and Dwyfor Davies, J. 'England and Wales: competition and control – or stakeholder and inclusion?', in *Inclusive Education*, H. Daniels and P. Garner (eds), London, Kogan Page, 1999.

Thomas, G., Walker, D. and Webb, J. *The Making of the Inclusive School*, London, Routledge, 1998.

Tuckman, B.W. and Jensen, M.A.C. 'Stages of small group development revisited', *Groups and Organisational Studies* 2, 1977, pp. 419–27.

Ward, J. and Le Dean, L. 'Student teachers' attitudes towards special education provision', *Educational Psychology* 16 (2), 1996, pp. 207–18.

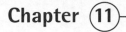
Roger Kidd

11.1 Introduction

From September 1978, when I became head of special educational needs at Chipping Norton comprehensive school, until my retirement from the post of Head of the East Riding Learning Support Service I was directly involved in three exciting and innovative integration schemes.

11.2 The three schemes

On my arrival at Chipping Norton I found that the provision for children with special needs took the format as a 'school within a school'. The special needs department catered for over seventy children all then classed as 'Educationally Subnormal'. Five classrooms were provided for the children, as were five teachers who remained with their class for over 80 per cent of the school week. Limited opportunities were provided for whole classes to leave the 'unit' for physical education and science but these lessons did not take place with children from the mainstream. The Warnock Report (DES, 1978) was published in the same year as my arrival at Chipping Norton and it was clear that this 'school within a school' had to become an integral part of the main school. However, in the not too distant past Chipping Norton school had been a grammar school and I quickly learnt that attitudes do not change overnight just because of the decree of a headteacher or a Local Education Authority (LEA). It involves a business of constant erosion, seizing opportunities when they occur and taking often small, albeit significant steps forward at the right time. In three years special needs provision at Chipping Norton had been transformed although there was more to be done and it was done after my departure. In 1981 I became head at Bishopswood School in South Oxfordshire. Bishopswood had opened in 1978 as a school for children with severe learning difficulties (SLD), many of the children transferring from Borocourt Hospital School. When local residents heard that Bishopswood was to be built on an isolated site close to a local primary school (Sonning Common) there was some opposition and protests were made. However, in spite of these protestations the school did open. By the time I left Bishopswood to move to Etton Pasture school in 1986 the majority of Bishopswood's pupils, apart from a small group of older children with profound and multiple difficulties (PMLD), were receiving their education in two mainstream schools:

Sonning Common primary school and Chiltern Edge comprehensive school. The children – whose arrival at the school on the isolated site close to the village had been the cause of some concern – were now included and valued members of the two other schools in the village (Kidd, 1984).

At the time of my departure, Oxfordshire LEA now accepted the need for all of Bishopswood's pupils, including older pupils with PMLD, to move into the mainstream. Bishopswood had always had a high proportion of these pupils. The agreed plan was for 'special care' facilities to be built at Chiltern Edge comprehensive school. Once ready, the final stage of the transfer of good practice would take place. Once this was completed, Bishopswood's building was sold to social services. Bishopswood school still exists with its own governing body and staff structure but all its operations take place in the accommodating mainstream schools.

Etton Pasture school in the East Riding of Yorkshire was a part-residential special school for children (age 5–16) with moderate learning difficulties (MLD). Due to the nature of its residential facilities children attended Etton Pasture from all four areas of what was then Humberside LEA. This occurred even though most children were from the East Riding area. I arrived at Etton Pasture as its new headteacher in September 1986. Events moved quickly and from September 1990 all children with MLD in the East Riding were to receive their education in mainstream schools. The special school, Etton Pasture, which had previously catered for these children, had closed at the end of the previous academic year. The children transferred to designated schools with located facilities, i.e. with additional staffing allocated by the East Riding Learning Support Service of which I was now headteacher (Northfield, 1988).

11.3 Meeting the requirements

The 1981 Education Act states that children with special educational needs (SEN) must be educated in ordinary schools subject to four conditions being met:

◆ parents' wishes must be taken into account;
◆ the child's special educational needs are properly catered for;
◆ that integration does not lead to an inefficient education for other children;
◆ that integration must lead to an efficient use of resources.

I shall consider each of these conditions in turn and, relying on my own experience of integrating children over many years, show that these conditions can be met. I would also propose therefore that they should not be seen as a barrier to the inclusion of the vast majority of children who are still attending special schools.

11.3.1 Parents' wishes must be taken into account

Most parents I have had contact with want mainstream provision for their child with SEN when they know that those needs could be properly provided for in mainstream. The problem arises when they are unaware that it is possible to meet these needs in mainstream settings.

The parents at Bishopswood School who saw their children transfer to the first Bishopswood classes at Sonning Common Primary School in 1981 and 1982 were generally very pleased about the development. Those who showed some concern were the parents of the children with PMLD who initially remained behind in the special school building. Their concern, and mine, was that their children were missing out on the stimulation and interaction they should have been receiving from their more able peers who were now in the Bishopswood classes in mainstream. The solution was obvious and these worries vanished when 'special care' type facilities were built in the mainstream and their children could now join their peers.

On arriving at Etton Pasture in September 1986 there was a commonly held belief among staff and parents that I had been appointed to close the school (oh, for such power!). My views on segregated special education had arrived before me and were well known. This rumour had to be quashed; if it was allowed to persist it could be damaging to morale. When trying to convince people that I could not possibly possess a mandate to close the school I reminded them that I had not closed Bishopswood, although the school had adopted an unusual way of working. I was, however, always keen to stress the advantages that inclusion could bring to children with special needs. My stance was the same as it had been previously at Bishopswood. If we could transfer to mainstream all that is better about a special school – such as its positive discrimination and its experience – then we could create what had at Bishopswood been described by parents as being 'the best of both worlds'. The advantages of a good special school are added to the major advantages resulting from the children attending a mainstream school and this is why they saw it as the best of both worlds. This stance was generally well received by the parents of children who attended Etton Pasture. However, some remained sceptical.

I could understand and sympathise with the anxieties of parents. In the past many had seen their children fail miserably in mainstream school. The transfer to the special school had brought happier times. There was also a belief that the LEA would not properly resource any inclusion project. There was also the view that they would use any attempt of an excuse to save money. I had always assured parents that I would be no party to that. Discussions confirmed what I always knew – that is, that any attempt to reintegrate these children would have to be carefully planned and properly resourced if the unhappiness of years ago was not to return. Parents would accept nothing less. I also knew that the correct attitude of teachers in mainstream was vital to success, as was the ethos of the receiving school; it really had to believe in accepting all its pupils as being of equal importance.

When the decision was finally made to close Etton and transfer its pupils to mainstream, all parents were visited by an education officer and myself. This was an opportunity to emphasise all the advantages of mainstream provision. I took some parents to observe good integrated provision already in existence. In the end twenty-seven out of twenty-nine sets of parents were happy with the transfer, subject to adequate resources being provided. Two sets of parents were not happy with the transfer but reluctantly agreed to it.

11.3.2 The child's special educational needs are properly catered for

My experience in Oxfordshire and Humberside shows that when integration schemes are properly resourced, the special needs of children can be properly met in mainstream provisions. In the case of Bishopswood school this included children with PMLD. However, there is no easy short cut and schemes have got to be well planned. Adequate preparation is essential. The Bishopswood scheme has been very successful. This had come about because we made sure that all that is good about a special school moved out with the children. After all, Bishopswood still exists albeit in mainstream schools. The position in the East Riding is less clear if measured by the satisfaction of the parents and their children who moved from Etton Pasture to the mainstream. Satisfaction appeared to be dependent on the philosophy of the receiving school and how they used their allocated additional resources.

About fourteen months after the closure of Etton Pasture I was asked by the Humberside LEA to carry out an evaluation of what had taken place

(Kidd and Hornby, 1993). This revealed that each of the six schools in the survey used its staff and organised its provision in different ways. Two schools, including the school that had the largest number of newly integrated pupils, decided that for the majority of the school week the pupils would receive their education in a special unit or resource base. However, the pupils were socially integrated as much as possible, for example, during tutor group activities and school assemblies.

The other four schools preferred to use staff mainly to support pupils in mainstream classes. In two of the schools *all* support was provided in-class. In the other two schools pupils were withdrawn from their mainstream classes for some of their time for individual or small group teaching sessions in addition to the provision of in-class support.

The ages of the children ranged from 8 to 16 with an average of approximately 13 years. Two children were transferred into a primary school and the others into one of five secondary schools. For the majority of the children these schools were not their local schools but were ones in which the LEA had decided to locate additional resources and staff.

Again, I interviewed all of the parents. I also interviewed the children individually at school. The main purpose of both sets of interviews was to establish whether or not they were happy about the transfer, regretted the transfer, or had no strong feelings either way. Therefore, after each interview the child or parent was categorised as being generally happy, neutral or as regretting the transfer.

11.3.3 Results of the survey

It was found that nineteen out of the twenty-nine parents (65 per cent) were happy with the transfer, six were neutral about it and four regretted the transfer. Similarly, twenty-two out of the twenty-nine children (76 per cent) were happy with the transfer, three were neutral about it and four regretted the transfer.

When the responses from parents whose children transferred to the school in which most of the teaching was conducted in the resource base were compared with those who transferred to one of the other four schools, a clear difference was observed. Eleven out of the twelve parents (92 per cent) whose children transferred to the resource-based teaching schools were happy with the transfer. They made comments such as 'It has worked out well, has really suited her... and been much better for her. She should never have gone to Etton Pasture.' Only one of the parents of these children was neutral and none regretted the transfer.

In contrast, only eight out of the seventeen parents (47 per cent) whose children attended the other schools were happy with the transfer, five of them were neutral, and four parents regretted the transfer. Comments included: 'He has had some bullying to put up with – mainly verbal but some physical. He seems to have more interests and more lessons. He preferred Etton Pasture because he had more trips out. Now he's in the classroom five days a week ... I'd have preferred a unit.'

Similarly, eleven out of the twelve children (92 per cent) who transferred to the resource-based teaching schools were happy with the transfer. One said: 'I like it here ... I wouldn't want to go back to Etton. We do more things here.' Only one of the children was neutral and none regretted the transfer.

However, only eleven out of the seventeen children (64 per cent) who transferred to the other schools were happy with the transfer, two were neutral about it and four of them regretted the transfer. One said: 'I miss all my friends. I am sometimes happy here but not all the time. I walk to school by myself ... people make fun of me and laugh.' In contrast, another who had also been picked on said he had 'reported it to a teacher and it was sorted out'.

Also, it was noted that, at one of the schools in which the pupils spent most of their time in mainstream classes, there was a difference between the pupils who were integrated individually and those who were placed in a mainstream class with other pupils from the special school. The level of satisfaction was greater for the three pupils (and their parents) who were grouped together in a mainstream class and who therefore could be supported for virtually all their lessons than for the other three pupils (and their parents) who were each integrated into different classes.

Thus, the findings of the survey suggest that there were generally greater levels of satisfaction among both parents and children, where the children were transferred to a school which used a mainly resource-based teaching model of integration, than in relation to children who attended the other schools. In addition, it seemed that pupils who were integrated into mainstream classes fared better when there were other children with learning difficulties in their classes. Although the numbers in the survey are too small for analysis to confirm that these differences are statistically significant, the pattern of responses appears to highlight a trend.

Further research was undertaken nearly ten years after the closure of Etton Pasture (Hornby and Kidd, 2001). Five of the original children and their parents could not be contacted but twenty-four were contacted and either the ex-pupils, parents, or both were interviewed.

A most important finding was the differences in the subject's views on their transfer to a more inclusive setting ten years earlier. The previous survey (Kidd and Hornby, 1993) had found that more of the students who were transferred into a unit within a mainstream school were satisfied than those moved into mainstream classes. The current survey found that this preference was maintained and was even stronger than before. Nearly all the subjects who spent their final years of secondary schooling in units within mainstream schools had found this experience helpful whereas the majority of subjects who were in mainstream classes had found it unhelpful.

However, the results of the studies do not necessarily support the adoption of more protective models of inclusion for children with MLD attending mainstream schools in the future. Since the majority of the children in the survey had spent several years in segregated special schools before transferring to mainstream schools, it is perhaps not surprising that many of them (and their parents) were happier with the kind of mainstream schooling which offered a relatively protective environment.

What is not clear from this research is whether more protective unit provision provides long-term advantages compared to in-class support models for children with MLD. More research needs to be undertaken and the problems of matching populations must not stop this from taking place.

11.3.4 Integration does not lead to an inefficient education for other children

I accept that there might well be a problem when the children to be integrated have substantial emotional and behavioural difficulties (EBD). However, there is no easy answer. Certainly it cannot be a sensible preparation for life to place up to seventy children with severe EBD together in a special school but I can accept that, for whatever reason, some children's difficulties are so severe that for them to remain in mainstream would be damaging to their peers. Fortunately, although a growth area, I am referring to very few children – a fraction of 1 per cent. However, those children from Etton Pasture and Bishopswood who received their education in mainstream have in no way led to an inefficient education for their mainstream peers. In fact, the presence of children with special needs in mainstream can considerably enrich and enhance the whole ethos of a school.

One of the most satisfying sights in my teaching career was to walk into the Bishopswood home base at Chiltern Edge comprehensive school one lunchtime and see two mainstream girls, with a Makaton signing manual in their hands, communicating with Sally – a girl who was autistic and who had no spoken language. I know of at least one mainstream volunteer from Chiltern Edge who, as a helper, accompanied Bishopswood children on a residential holiday and was so motivated that she decided on a career working with people with learning difficulties. The headteacher of Chiltern Edge at the time told me that, to him, the biggest advantage of the presence of Bishopswood children at Chiltern Edge was the awareness of disability it developed in his pupils.

11.3.5 Integration must lead to an efficient use of resources

This condition can be used as a 'cop out' for those LEAs and perhaps some special school staff who wish to preserve the segregated system. Special schools do exist and therefore children will be found to dispatch to them – if not, it can be argued that it is an inefficient use of resources to have empty places. The result is that the expensive human resource they contain remains locked in the special school. I believe it is the dual system that leads to the inefficient use of resources, i.e. special schools and token attempts to integrate. What is required is a more radical stance. Etton Pasture School was an example of that. The decision was made, largely because its headteacher and Governors wanted it to be made. They wanted to close the special school and provide for the children in well-resourced mainstream provision. A date was set, the locked up resources were moved out to mainstream and the children moved with them.

11.4 Conclusion

I do worry. What has happened to the brave new world that many of us thought was heralded by the Warnock Report (DES, 1978) and the 1981

Education Act? In the mid-1980s, I wrote to the educational press stating that: '*In the twenty-first century educationalists will look back in anger at a system that allowed children with disabilities to be removed from their schools and bussed to a special school, some being removed from their families when the bussing was to a residential special school.*'

The twenty-first century has arrived and separate provision still exists. However, if we have at last reached the time when no new segregated special schools are opened, that will be progress. My experience tells me that, apart possibly from those children with severe behavioural difficulties, all children with special needs can be successfully educated in mainstream when all the advantages of a good special school are to be found there. However, I do feel that for those children with the most severe problems some grouping, albeit in a mainstream school, will always be required and attendance at the *local* mainstream school will not be possible for all. The jury is still out on what type of provision in mainstream is most appropriate for the largest group, those with MLD. Research might well indicate that a myriad of provision is required.

In many ways the inclusion of children with SLD may prove to be initially easier than inclusion for children with MLD. I have found that a natural sympathy exists for children with SLD that unfortunately does not necessarily extend to the pupils with MLD who are perceived to look comparatively 'normal'.

Throughout this chapter I have emphasised that, to be successful, inclusion projects must ensure that the expertise, positive discrimination and the commitment of the teachers found in a good special school must be apparent in the mainstream school. Of equal importance is the need for the mainstream school to accept that all its pupils are of equal value. My most recent survey of ex-pupils and their parents indicated that these prerequisites were not always met when the children from Etton Pasture transferred to mainstream in 1990.

Many parents reported that whereas advice, support and contact with other agencies were always forthcoming when the child was attending the special school, this was not always the case after the transfer to mainstream schools. Parents praised the 'Annual Review' system that I had introduced at Etton, but what followed in mainstream schools was not always so helpful. The parents of a child with special needs often need the support that a good special school can give. It is possible that support is even more vital when their child is included and assimilated into a large mainstream school – while some peers can be friendly, others can be unkind. Six ex-pupils reported to me that they had been bullied on their arrival in the mainstream. Only one of the six that mentioned bullying was a pupil at the secondary school where most teaching was carried out in a home base. The parents of this child reported that when this did occur at the school the headteacher spoke to the whole school about disability and the need to value all people. The five who felt they were at the receiving end of bullying at other schools felt that nothing had been done about it. Interestingly, and to my surprise, no child reported having been teased or bullied by other children from their neighbourhood when they had been bussed to the special school.

Very few ex-students of Etton reported to having been placed on work experience from their mainstream schools. When work experience had been provided, it was often for a very short time and the preparation for the placement was often poor. One parent reported to me how her daughter had been sent on a placement to some stables without adequate preparation and the girl was so shy and embarrassed that serious problems arose when she needed to use the toilet. If the children had remained at Etton they would have been the recipients of an excellent preparation for work course including well-prepared and executed work experience.

The most worrying incident I heard about during the year 2000 survey came from the mother of an ex-pupil. Her son had transferred to a school where most support was given away from a resource base. The son and parents, although initially pleased with the transfer, became disillusioned with the reality. The mother reported that there were several problems giving rise to concern including teasing. At a parents meeting one of the teachers responsible for SEN, who had been appointed because of the transfer from Etton Pasture, said to the mother 'after all, let's be honest, he shouldn't be here'. No wonder the parents now consider the whole venture to have been damaging. In desperation the mother even approached the neighbouring LEA to see whether her son could transfer to one of its MLD special schools! Let's hope that others will learn from those mistakes. Inclusion can work and where it does it is better than segregation.

References

Department for Education and Science *Special Educational Needs: Report of the Committee of Enquiry into the Education of Handicapped Children and Young People*, London, HMSO, 1978.

Hornby, G. and Kidd, R. 'Transfer from special to mainstream: ten years later', *British Journal of Special Education* 28 (1), 2001, pp. 10–17.

Kidd, R. *Transferring Good Practice*, Bristol, CSIE, 1994.

Kidd, R. and Hornby, G. 'Transfer from special to mainstream', *British Journal of Special Education* 20 (1), 1993, pp. 17–19.

Northfield, V. *Good Practice Transferred*, Bristol, CSIE, 1988.

Charles Gains

12.1 Inclusive scenarios

Khadijah is 7 years old and her brain was damaged at birth. As a consequence of this she suffers from cortical blindness, physical and complex learning difficulties. For some years she attended a special school for the blind. However, her parents became determined that she should attend her local mainstream school. Eventually an agreement was reached that she could spend two days at her special school and three at her local mainstream school – with a full-time learning support assistant (LSA). Additionally, she was to receive help from therapists and a visiting specialist in visual impairment. Her class teacher, Heidi, is very experienced and has a particular interest in disability. After initial difficulties, Khadijah has settled in very well indeed and is included in all curriculum activities. She is a lively child, popular with classmates and has acquired a few close friends. She represents a fine example of successful inclusion and will shortly transfer to a full-time mainstream placement.

James is 6 years of age and has come through the school's nursery. His statement indicates that he has a 'complex learning difficulty' although staff descriptions of him as 'autistic' may well be nearer the mark. He has little interaction with other pupils and his behaviour is frequently described as 'bizarre'. He acts impulsively, shouts out and disrupts lessons occasionally. However, other pupils have adjusted to this and it causes little bother for them. He has a full-time LSA and works from an individual but parallel programme to his classmates. The local education authority (LEA) provides him with additional speech therapy and a member of its support team oversees his programme. James' parents are very involved in his education and the school has an excellent relationship with them. Harry, his teacher, is young and enthusiastic and has carefully researched James' difficulties. He has also sought appropriate professional guidance. But even given the additional help, he finds James' presence hard work and wonders what will happen as James grows older and his behaviour becomes less socially acceptable.

Emma is 9 years of age and has a growing behaviour problem. She is extremely disruptive and attention seeking. She needs constant supervision, even in the playground where she appears to set out to deliberately spoil other children's activities. Although she has been in the school several years and her behaviour has been contained, there are signs that it is becoming more exaggerated and dangerous. Her parents will not accept there is a problem and insist that she is 'dyslexic'. However, the local authority educational psychologist found she did not meet any of the criteria for dyslexia and no statement was issued. Clare, her teacher, is mature and very experienced. She has dealt with similar problems before but is in total despair when it comes to Emma. The perceived stubbornness of Emma's father and mother is making the situation intolerable. Clare is aware of the mutterings among other parents about Emma's deteriorating behaviour and the disruption to their own children's education. In desperation the school is considering its first exclusion.

All three of these children present very different challenges to teachers. Given the ever-increasing range of learning difficulties being catered for in mainstream schools it may come as little surprise that these pupils all attend the same school. 'St Optimas CE' is a primary school in a small Midlands town, which is neither 'inner city' nor 'leafy suburb'. Although once famous for its engineering works the town owes its economic survival to the development of a modest business and retail park and its relatively easy commuter access to a principal city. The school draws on a still significant town-centre core of Victorian properties, a large pre-war council estate and an outer circle of owner-occupier estates. St Optimas is mainly housed in 1960s-style buildings although its history goes back to 1880. It is an institution held in high regard in the community and is over-subscribed because parents openly state that they value its high standards and Christian ethos.

About 2 per cent of the school's population has a statement of special educational needs (SEN), with a further 15 per cent deemed as having SEN. The headteacher is very committed and the staff are of a very high standard. Several teachers have foregone promotion in order to remain in such a productive and supportive environment. OfSTED reports have been extremely favourable and particularly positive about the school's policy regarding SEN. However, the school makes no claim to be better than countless numbers of primary schools either locally or nationally.

The children mentioned, and the school itself, are real-life situations: only names have been changed. They illustrate some of the issues that are bound to arise in a 'full inclusion' scenario. A primary school is used here as an example as it is often markedly different from a secondary school where resources might be more liberal. Khadijah is regarded, quite rightly, as an excellent example of inclusion. James typifies many aspects of good inclusive practice: supportive and understanding parents, a well-managed and staffed school, and the availability of additional and specialised help. However, limitations are anticipated in the long term. Emma, on the other hand, has tested this flexible school to the limit and is on course for inclusion breakdown.

12.2 Observations

Distant observers and crude analysts, and we appear to have an abundance of these, might argue that if a school can tackle one case successfully, as in the case of Khadijah, it should be able to handle an infinite number of children with SEN. This is nonsense – an insult to the ongoing efforts of teachers who struggle to sustain as many pupils as they can in mainstream. I call the capacity of a school to deal with difference in its many forms its *inclusive infrastructure*, a complex and ever-changing capacity of an institution to respond to challenge. The key elements of an inclusive infrastructure I would describe as attitudes, personnel, resources, involvement and logistics (APRIL). Additionally, there are factors that are completely outside the control of schools, e.g. poverty and social disadvantage, which present insuperable difficulties in spite of what the Minister for Education and Her Majesty's Chief Inspector of Schools would have us believe. Even such patently successful schools as St Optima's will have their fracture points unless they completely revise their *raison d'être* as a school for all children.

It seems incredible that far-reaching policies have been introduced without information and debate. Operating from a legitimate, but what I would consider restricted view of human rights, the full inclusion lobby has invaded all major channels of administration to such a degree that disagreement has been marginalised and individual doubts suppressed. It is perhaps overstating matters but there does appear to be a reluctance to express a different view to that of the establishment for fear one might be labelled 'anti-inclusion'. I will risk that disapprobation. It does appear to be beyond my comprehension, for example, that in order to show political correctness, countless thousands of children representing the vast range of learning difficulties are being 'shoe-horned' into mainstream schools with little or no help. The chemical crutch of Ritalin is a case in point. The ill-conceived and largely indiscriminate use of this drug is driven in good part by a desire to make some pupils amenable to 'inclusion' no matter what long-term effects this might have for themselves or anybody else.

It seems to me that without any real attempt to research inclusive strategies, or to examine and debate the implications critically, we have stumbled into a morass of thankfully good practice but also with a fair leavening of mediocrity and, in some cases, mayhem. The beneficial results, and there are many examples, are paraded with accompanying exhortations but the, as yet, unquantifiable number of 'failures' are mainly ignored. If not ignored, they are simply put down to teacher incompetence, indifference or hostility. This level of debate is frustrating to those of us who want inclusive practices to spread but within an ordered and intelligent framework. I will argue, if only to clarify thinking, that there is a need to return to the rationale, arguments and delivery of inclusive education rather than continuing to stagger aimlessly towards some messy conclusion.

12.3 Decisions

Elsewhere, with Philip Garner, I have attempted to outline the parameters a constructive debate might take (Garner and Gains, 2000). These are summarised in Table 12.1. Writers and observers regularly return to the definitive Salamanca Statement (UNESCO, 1994). This is undoubtedly a landmark document in the world of SEN and clearly sets out arguments for inclusion in terms of human rights. It has had justifiably, a coherent and powerful impact on policy and provision and takes a very positive stand in relation to equity, empowerment and enablement. Nevertheless, it raises as many questions as it appears to resolve. For example, a common dilemma occurs when the education of a single pupil appears to impede or even damage the education of his/her contemporaries. Emma is a case in point. Likewise there will be, at any time, societal aspirations and demands that affect schools and attempt to pull them in conflicting directions. Add to this a lack of agreement on what inclusion really means, and the case put by strict adherents to the Salamanca directive finds itself under some pressure. Given all this, I conclude that current pressures to include are externally driven and based largely on political and ideological demands rather than cool and informed consideration. In my opinion this *mélange* invites disaster.

Table 12.1 Concepts, constraints and outcomes

Concepts	Constraints	Outcomes
Human rights		
Issues	Issues	Debate is top-down,
equity	rights for 'all'	externally driven
empowerment	definition	Based on political/
enablement	societal limitations	ideological rather
		than individual need
Delivery		
Issues	Issues	Shift to mainstream
knowledge	training	inclusion acceptable
management	resources	but dependent on
		crucial
		pre-conditions
The curriculum		
Issues	Issues	Lack of flexibility
quality	National Curriculum rigidity	
particular need	assessment/inspection	

In terms of delivery, there are similar unresolved problems. Inclusion demands a high level of knowledge and the sophisticated management of resources. The constraints here are self-evident. Initial teacher training and the subsequent updating of school staff in the field of special educational needs are little short of a national scandal (Robertson, 1999; Garner, 2001). In spite of sometimes heroic attempts to absorb and deal with complex behaviour and learning difficulty, there are clearly many otherwise competent teachers who regularly find themselves 'out of their depth'. It is ironic that they then are liable to suffer criticism from those whom First World War poet Siegfried Sassoon might describe as living *'with scarlet Majors at the Base'* and speeding *'glum heroes up the line to death'*. Additionally, there are suggestions that the move to inclusion is not only badly thought out but also inadequately resourced. Mainstream provision, even with additional in-class support, is still a much cheaper option than special schooling. It is not surprising that it appeals to decision-makers and public accountants. I conclude that while I welcome the moves towards mainstream inclusion, there are crucial pre-conditions that will determine its successful outcome.

The final element of the 'debate' centres on the school curriculum. Here, children with SEN need to be assured of quality provision and matching need. The intention of a National Curriculum was to offer a standard package to all, irrespective of their ability or disability. A worthy aim but this can place severe constraints on tackling the specific needs of an individual. Currently, the argument is being revisited as to the suitability, or otherwise, of a standard cognitive package however imaginatively presented. As Hornby (2001) says *'inclusion in an unsuitable curriculum directly contributes to the disaffection of many pupils'*. It almost goes without saying that the current government obsession with pupil and school assessment, league tables and OfSTED inspections is hardly likely to encourage schools to welcome different or difficult pupils or, subsequently, experiment with more creative delivery systems. Unhappily I conclude that there is increasingly a lack of willingness or opportunity to experiment, a feature that flourished in times of less prescription and interference.

12.4 Routes

I would argue that no two individual's needs are ever exactly the same and echo the view of Tod (2001) who states *'the individual appears to have been forgotten in the planning of the inclusion process'*. It is obvious that while two children might share a recognisable problem in relation to their schooling, in terms of temperament they could be poles apart. The one might be happily absorbed and included in all aspects of school life, the other could react quite differently, even disruptively. To impose an adult perspective on placement, however well intentioned, could turn out to be extremely damaging for the individual concerned. Hornby takes a very robust view of this scenario:

> *'The level of inclusion, either locational, social or functional, should be decided on the needs of each individual child and the exigencies of each situation. Once the necessity for this is accepted, then the focus of special educators can return to that of meeting the individual needs of children with SEN rather than attempting to make "one size fit all".'*

1999, p. 157

Inclusive practice appears to me to fall into three broad categories. First, there is *traditional inclusion*. Traditional inclusion has been around since schooling began. Although special schools took up what was then deemed 'handicaps', many children, particularly those with mild or moderate learning difficulties, remained in the mainstream situation. The classic solutions were somewhat crude and consisted of streaming, setting, special classes, withdrawal groups, and so on. While these presented teachers with some problems, they fell largely within their normal expectations and expertise. Their training had given them some insight, albeit limited. Some practitioners even came to enjoy working with 'slow learners', gained expertise and went on to specialise. Ramshackle though all of this appeared to be, it was not without some virtue.

Second, *responsible inclusion*. This is a term used by Vaughn and Schumm (1995) which I shall borrow. Responsible inclusion appeared, originating from the Warnock Report (DES, 1978) and subsequent legislation, and was accompanied by a readiness within the profession to absorb wider categories of disability and learning difficulty. The most obvious beneficiaries were children with physical problems, those with hearing or sight impairment, and children with Down's Syndrome, for example. Teacher awareness had grown, supplemented with additional support and resources in the classroom. Then, as now, the major stumbling block to the comprehensive adoption of a full inclusion strategy lay in the areas of complex disability and 'bizarre' behaviour. Responsible inclusion had proceeded sensibly if somewhat erratically.

The cumulative effect of legislation, over the past twelve years, has turned a stroll into a stampede. Under increased pressure from government and its OfSTED agents, LEAs have begun the dismantling of their special school structures and the consequent absorption of pupils with SEN into mainstream schools. There are many instances where this has gone extremely well and examples of good practice have enjoyed the publicity they deserve. However, expectations had been raised, particularly among parents, that schools could competently deal with almost any learning difficulty. It is now becoming clear that there are limits to the exercise and that there are pupils whose needs cannot be easily met in mainstream, even given generous support. Containment in these circumstances has taken precedence over education. Where such instances occur I would deem this to be *forced inclusion,* i.e. included in superficial terms that may satisfy the casual enquirer but in reality frustrating to the individual child and a burden on the school. The inclusive infrastructure, referred to earlier, has been tested to destruction.

There are, it appears to me, three routes available. The first is to retain the special school network. Expansion is unacceptable for several reasons although rationalisation of existing resources is called for and appears to be proceeding reasonably well. The second pathway, encouraged by an influential and significant lobby, would have us go 'hell for leather' towards full inclusion notwithstanding the consequences and learn to cope as circumstances dictate. It is clear that I find this route repugnant, as it seems to find acceptable casualties on all sides. I am more comfortable looking at the 'middle way' as represented by 'responsible inclusion' the principles of which have been laid out by Vaughn and Schumm (1995).

12.5 Destination

In the field of SEN briefly traced views have changed and expertise has evolved over the last two decades. The large increase of pupils that are 'included' is to be warmly welcomed. But as I have indicated we seem, at times, to be stretching ourselves well beyond the parameters of existing knowledge and expertise. I would contend that there are, and will always be, limits to full inclusion and we deceive others, and ourselves certainly in the short to medium term, if we maintain otherwise.

It seems that some observers and writers regularly miss the point when they argue for full inclusion in schools. As Hornby (2001) wryly observes *'inclusion in the community is the actual end that educators are seeking. Inclusion in mainstream school may be a means to that end but it is not the end in itself.'* An education that is different from mainstream *may* prove a handicap in later life. That is debatable. What we do know, at least from the increasing numbers of young people 'switching off', is that the present curriculum is not working for significant numbers (Davies, 2000). What matters is a relevant and challenging curriculum for youngsters and the location, I would argue, is of secondary importance.

12.6 Coda

How best can I summarise all this? I offer ten points for consideration.

1 The inclusion debate is not over, as some observers would have us believe, indeed, it never took place.

2   We know very little about the practical implementation of inclusive
    strategies, the current discourse rages around ideological and political
    viewpoints with little in the way of substantial research and hard
    evidence.

3   Inclusion can take many forms and is not simply about locating or re-
    locating pupils in mainstream classes.

4   A school can still deem itself 'inclusive' even if it subscribes to a variety
    of internal strategies that outside observers may label otherwise.

5   Each school has a capacity for inclusion that will vary according to its
    APRIL (attitudes, personnel, resources, involvement and logistics)
    infrastructure.

6   The crucial element for inclusion lies within each teacher, indicating
    considerably more input into teacher training and re-training.

7   Inclusive schooling is a means to an end not the end in itself – which is
    inclusion in society.

8   'Responsible inclusion' as a concept offers more than crude and
    simplistic solutions. It offers sensible policies for implementing school-
    based practice.

9   The *ad hoc* dismantling of special schools should be accompanied by a
    major re-think of support for pupils in a variety of situations.

10 Inclusive education is part of a wider transformation of education,
    which already sees countless numbers of children alienated from the
    system.

In summary, I see inclusion in terms of a sporting metaphor. The outgoing
relay runner has started too soon and searches desperately for the
incoming runner's baton. Unsurprisingly the baton is not taken, even
dropped. The race, of course, is over unless the baton is quickly reclaimed.
There is little point in the outgoing runner sprinting away, however
flamboyantly they manage to do so. Special needs provision relies on
similar teamwork and continuity but, I would contend, the take-over has
been fumbled. Time to recover the baton?

References

Davies, N. 'The tower block children for whom school has no point', *The
    Guardian*, 10 July, 2000.

Department for Education and Science *Special Educational Needs: Report
    of the Committee of Enquiry into the Education of Handicapped Children
    and Young People,* London, HMSO, 1978.

Garner, P. 'Goodbye Mr Chips', Chapter 4 in this volume, 2001.

Garner, P. and Gains, C. 'Inclusion: the debate that never happened', *Special!* Autumn, 2000, pp. 8–11.

Hornby, G. 'Inclusion or delusion: can one size fit all?' *Support for Learning* 14 (4), 1999, pp. 152–7.

Hornby, G. 'Promoting responsible inclusion: Quality education for all', Chapter 1 in this volume, 2001.

Robertson, C. 'Initial teacher education and inclusive schooling', *Support for Learning* 14 (4), 1999, pp. 169–73.

Tod, J. 'Enabling inclusion for individuals', Chapter 2 in this volume, 2001.

UNESCO *The Salamanca Statement and Framework for Action on Special Needs Education*, New York, UNESCO, 1994.

Vaughn, S. and Schumm, J.S. 'Responsible inclusion for students with learning disabilities', *Journal of Learning Disabilities* 28 (5), 1995, pp. 264–70.

Tim O'Brien

Throughout this book areas for critical questioning and debate have been analysed and explored in order to take us beyond current inclusive practice. In this chapter, I shall outline the key emerging issues.

13.1 Definitions of inclusion

There are still confusions associated with the meaning of inclusion. There appears to be a lack of a mutual meaning in terms of conceptualisation and application. Different people use the term in different ways and with varying attitudinal intentions. Definitions of inclusion have altered, and will alter, as cultural and societal changes occur. There is confusion about what 'full inclusion' actually means and how it might be operationalised in the educational system. It is unclear as to whether full inclusion requires one system for all or a combination of interrelated inclusive systems. Consideration has to be given to the implications for all pupils if inclusion is intended to be a means to an end rather than an end in itself. Fundamentally, inclusion seems to be both a fragile and unstable concept.

13.2 Models of inclusion

No single model can assure that individuals will take up their right to quality education. There is a naïvety in the application of a singular model and this may be compounded by elements of inherent naïvety within the models themselves. Gaining an insight into the complexities inherent in these models, and the implications for developing practice, will not be achieved by the chanting of mantras or polarised, aggressive and inflexible standpoints. In striving towards enabling the conditions for 'inclusion for all' to flourish we might conclude that traditional models that address notions of disaffection and disability may not be sufficient for enabling inclusion. For example, a synthesis drawing on the psychological, biological and social models could take the inclusion debate beyond the realms of technical rationalism. Explanatory frameworks, some of which remain flawed and reductionist, must be referenced to empirical understanding.

13.3 The process of inclusion

Enabling inclusion is not a mechanistic phenomenon and process – it has real human consequences for pupils, teachers, parents and advocates. The process of inclusion is currently being hindered by an educational climate that places such a heavy emphasis on market-force competition between pupils and schools and the failure of pupils and teachers to meet externally prescribed criteria. New visions and radical solutions will be required if we are to change an educational system that has historically promoted segregation and exclusive practice. Recent legislative decisions have reinforced exclusivity. We have to remain aware of the climate and conditions for change and whether they facilitate, mediate or hinder inclusion. For many learners there is a discrepancy between the philosophy of inclusion and the process and practice as they experience it. It is legitimate that the rights of children are central to the inclusion process. However, there are conflicts between standpoints that are established within the parameters of human or moral rights. These can result in confusions about who is enabled to make choices and what strategies for inclusion should be adopted and accepted and by whom.

13.4 Outcome research

An extensive base of research on inclusion does not exist. That which does exist does not provide a uniformly positive picture. By applying what is learned from outcome research we can improve inclusive provision in schools and in classrooms. Without data all that we have are assumptions about the benefits or disadvantages of inclusion. Research will be required concerning those pupils for whom inclusion, in reality, means exclusion. This includes pupils who experience difficulties in collaborative learning, those who have a negative impact upon the learning of others often due to emotional and behavioural difficulties (EBD) and those who opt out of mainstream provision. Further research would also provide an insight into how inclusive practice could be implemented for the population of pupils who currently carry the label 'severe and complex difficulties'. It is likely that a combination of qualitative and quantitative measures will be necessary to gain data about outcomes for individuals and groups. There needs to be awareness that there could be a substantial difference between outcomes for individuals and groups because the context, details and outcomes of one inclusion scenario will be different from the next.

13.5 Curriculum issues

Being included in the school building is one level, a superficial level, of inclusion. It is only one component of an inclusive infrastructure and appears to be no different to a model of locational integration. The key to inclusion is the provision of inclusive learning. To achieve inclusive learning pupils must be included in the curriculum. If flexible placement arrangements are to be the way forward, allowing pupils to move back and forth between special and mainstream schools, curriculum issues have to be at the forefront of professional consideration. Issues such as curriculum specialisation, balance and justification will need to remain under constant review, as will issues of pedagogy, especially concerning how it can connect with learners in newly constructed inclusive contexts. Systematic evaluation of approaches to educating pupils with SEN should be undertaken so that we can establish which approaches provide quality learning. Schools will then be required to reappraise the balance and relevance of the curriculum so that they ensure that inclusive placement recognises the individuality of all pupils. We cannot assume that because someone is included within a mainstream school that this will become a guarantee of successful learning.

13.6 Professional resources

The key to enabling inclusion lies within the teacher. We can no longer continue with the process of imposing new regimes upon teachers who have not been offered relevant professional development and who consequently encounter a shortfall of skills. We must provide systems where officially sanctioned and resourced professional development and awareness raising – at all levels – can occur for these teachers. What about those who are training to be teachers in a new and inclusive educational world? We are still uncertain of the national picture regarding the exposure to inclusion issues that occurs during initial teacher training (ITT) both in and out of the classroom. Why do we still know so little about what is really occurring in ITT in relation to training teachers in SEN/inclusive provision? When assessing teacher-training provision we have to consider why special schools have effectively been marginalised from the teacher training process.

13.7 Dispersal of knowledge, skills and understanding

The case against special schools is not yet a proven one. If special schools are to continue to exist, they must be enabled to provide clearly defined and mutually beneficial learning links with mainstream schools. This equitable approach allows for the sharing and growth of mutual expertise. There is much evidence of good practice within special schools and this has to be disseminated in a reciprocal fashion with colleagues in mainstream schools. Curriculum development, not curriculum mimicry, is the way forward. Systems need to become less protective and isolated and more open to change.

13.8 Stakeholder consultation

The main stakeholders in the inclusion process need to become more explicitly involved in it. Their multiple voices are of great importance and are largely unheard at the moment. Top-down and 'outside in' approaches have a tendency to impose change and develop systems without consultation. This has an impact upon morale and may create situations where new initiatives are not understood. It does not provide the conditions for empowering pupils, parents and teachers and for enabling inclusion. Centrally driven policies need to recognise the relentless inequality that some individuals feel and experience both in and out of school. Over recent years practice has developed for addressing individual needs. This includes the provision of learning support within school, learning support from outside the school (therapy, educational psychology) and tools such as the individual education plan (IEP). If individuals are to be beneficiaries of inclusion, such practice has to be targeted to current and emerging needs. It should also be contextualised and clarified so that it can be evaluated in relation to outcomes. The subjective experience of learners should never be disregarded and nor should their individual needs become secondary to ideological commitment. This ensures that those who are alienated by the system do not disappear from the system. It could also enable those who may experience problems gaining full access to the system – such as members of travelling communities, refugees or asylum seekers – to become included.

13.9 Breaking the negative cycle

If inclusion is to benefit all learners, then models and ideologies have to be analysed. Historically, definitions in the area of special educational needs (SEN) have been rooted in psychological and medical discourses. The social model challenged some of the underlying assumptions associated with these discourses. Models need to be open to critique and there needs to be greater dialogue across differing perspectives. Before current practice and systems are deconstructed, by a move towards full inclusion, we have to evaluate differing models and gain data. This offers both the opportunity to retain good practice and to acknowledge that the prior experiences and dispositions of those involved, while potentially open to change, are extremely significant.

We also need to gain data regarding the efficacy of inclusive practice. A climate where the conditions for creating suspicion, fear or excessive competition is prevalent and promoted is counterproductive in operationalising and evaluating inclusion.

In this book, reservations have been expressed about how cultural and educational reform is being managed and developed in schools in the United Kingdom and the United States and its implications in relation to enabling inclusion. The consequences of not recognising the inherent complexity of enabling inclusion can be represented in the negative cycle shown in figure 13.1.

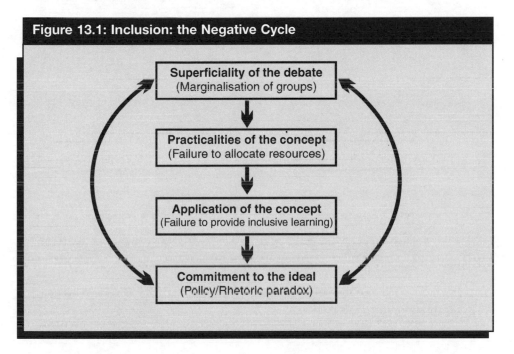

Figure 13.1: Inclusion: the Negative Cycle

One aim of this book is to break this cycle at the earliest point: to generate a more critical debate, to discuss the values and assumptions associated with inclusion, so that all learners can be included in whatever system meets their diverse needs. The inclusion debate – as exemplified by some of the themes and dilemmas raised in this book – is in its earliest stages. Let it continue ...